DRAGON 32

programmer's reference guide

Contents

DRAGON 32
programmer's reference guide

JOHN VANDER REYDEN

MELBOURNE HOUSE

First Published in 1983 by Melbourne House

This Remastered Edition
Published in 2021 by
Acorn Books
www.acornbooks.co.uk

This book is a page-by-page reproduction of the original 1983 edition as published by Melbourne House. The entirety of the book is presented with no changes, corrections nor updates to the original text, images and layout save for a renumbering of the pages; therefore no guarantee is offered as to the accuracy of the information within.

INTRODUCTION

This book has been developed as a reference source for people like you, who want to get the most out their DRAGON. It contains the information you need for your programs, from the simplest exercises right though to complex business or game applications. The DRAGON PROGRAMMERS GUIDE is designed so that everyone from the beginning BASIC programmer to the professional experienced 6809 machine language programmer can get information to develop their own creative programs. At the same time this book shows you just what your DRAGON can do.

This PROGRAMMERS GUIDE is not designed to teach the BASIC programming language to a beginner but as a reference to the DRAGON which includes the DRAGON's BASIC language. If you have not already done some programming, I suggest that you read the other book in this series, THE COMPLETE DRAGON BASIC COURSE, which will teach you the BASIC language.

The DRAGON PROGRAMMER'S GUIDE is just that; a guide. Like most reference books, your ability to apply the information depends on your knowledge of the subject. In other words, if you are a novice programmer you will not be able to use all the facts and figures in this book until your knowledge and experience increases.

What is in this book is a considerable amount of valuable programming reference material written in easy to read English with the programming jargon explained. On the other hand, the programming professional will find all the information needed to use the capabilities of the DRAGON 32 effectively.

WHAT'S INCLUDED?

- Complete "BASIC dictionary" includes the DRAGON BASIC language commands, statements and functions, a detailed description of each word and examples on how to use it, even the average time it takes to execute each one, useful for "time critical" game programs.
- An introduction to machine code programming and how to use machine code programs from BASIC.
- A complete listing of the 6809 instruction set.
- The peripherals chapter (Chapter 5) shows how the DRAGON can communicate with the outside world via its ports.
- Useful routines and memory locations you can access from both BASIC and machine code
- BASIC and machine code routines for you to type in yourself which will make your program even more powerful and user friendly.

HOW TO USE THIS GUIDE

Throughout this manual certain conventional notations are used to describe the syntax (programming sentence structure) of BASIC commands to show both the required and the optional parts for each keyword. The rules to use for interpreting statments' syntax are as follows:

- BASIC keywords are shown in capital letters. They must appear where shown in the statement, entered and spelled exactly as shown.
- Parameter names are shown enclosed in square brackets ([ ]) and these must be substituted with values. These can be either a single constant, a single variable name or any complex expression unless otherwise stated.
- TIME - Most commands have a time quoted for them at the end of their description. This is the approximate average time that the command takes to run, measured in seconds. It is included to enable comparison of different ways of performing a certain routine when programming time-critical programs.

CHAPTER 1

BASIC

This chapter is a reference guide to the DRAGON 32's BASIC. If you are new to programming then I suggest that you use a book like THE COMPLETE DRAGON BASIC COURSE which is written for people who don't have a lot of BASIC programming experience. If you are a competent programmer but have not used BASIC before, this chapter is probably sufficient to teach you the basics of the BASIC language.

CONSTANTS

DRAGON BASIC has two fundamental types of constants; string and numeric.

String constants are made up of alphanumeric characters and are enclosed in quotation marks (""). A character string can be up to 255 characters long. A string which does not contain any characters is called a "null string".
Examples:
"DRAGON 32"
"!!23!"
"m"
"" - null string

Numeric constants can have three formats:
a) DECIMAL
These can contain the digits 0 through 9, a decimal point (.) and a sign (+ or −).
Example:
−2783.796, 1200
Decimal numbers can also be stored in EXPONENTIAL FORMAT and are automatically displayed in this format for numbers greater than 1,000 million and less than 1 thousandth. The highest value the exponent can take is 38; actually the largest number is about 1.1×10^{38}. The mantissa has a maximum of 9 digits.
Example:
9.76E13, −9.67E−21

b) HEXIDECIMAL
These can contain the digits 0 through to 9, A through to F and a sign (+ or −), where:
A represents 10
B represents 11
C represents 12

D represents 13
E represents 14
F represents 15
"&H" is placed at the start of the number to indicate that it is in hexadecimal format. If a sign is specified then it must come before "&H".
Example:
&H1A00, −&H1A0F

c) OCTAL
These can contain 0 through to 7 and a sign (+ or −). "&" or "&O" is placed at the start of the number to indicate that it is an octal number. If a sign is specified it must be placed at the very head of the number.
Example:
&O707, −&O707, &147

VARIABLES
Again, the DRAGON has two types of variables, string and numeric, the only difference being that all numeric variables are floating point. A variable need not be declared unless it is an array with more than 10 elements.

Variable names have the following rules:
a) The first character must be alphabetic (A - Z) followed by alphanumeric characters.
b) Up to 255 characters may be used as a name but only the first 2 are used to identify the variable. Therefore, SNAKE and SNAP are considered the same by the DRAGON.
c) Variable names cannot start with a BASIC keyword.
Examples:
ABCD, IDATA, INPRINT2 - correct
1DARE, DATA1, TOM - incorrect
String variables are signified by a dollar sign ($) added at the end of their names. Up to 255 characters can be stored by any one string variable.

Whenever a program is RUN or changes made to the program, string variables are initialized to the null string, and numeric variables to 0.

ARRAYS
An array is a group, or table of values with the same variable name. Individual values (called elements) are referenced by subscript(s) of numeric expressions. Multiple dimensioned arrays are available and the number of subscripts must agree with the number of dimensions that the array was declared with (see the DIM statement).

CONVERSION

When a constant of hexadecimal or octal format is assigned to a numeric variable, or printed, it is automatically converted to a floating point number. String constants or variables cannot be mixed directly with numeric variables and constants but there are functions for this purpose.

EXPRESSIONS

The following is the formal priority or execution sequence in BASIC numeric expressions, their symbols and function:

1. Parenthesis	( )	Give sub-expressions higher execution priority
2. Functions		(see pages 28-35)
3. Arithmetic operators	÷	Exponentation e.g. 2 ↑ 3 = 2^3
	−	make numbers negative
	*	Multiplication
	/	Division
	+	Addition
	−	Subtraction
4. Relational operators	=	Equivilence
	< >, > <	Not equal
	<	less than
	>	greater than
	< =, = <	less than or equal to
	> =, = >	greater than or equal to

5. Logical Operators

NOT (negation)	X	NOT X	
	true (−1)	false (0)	
	false (0)	true (−1)	
OR (logical add)	X	Y	X OR Y
	true (−1)	true (−1)	true (−1)
	true (−1)	false (0)	true (−1)
	false (0)	true (−1)	true (−1)
	false (0)	false (0)	false (0)
AND (logical multiply)	X	Y	X AND Y
	true (−1)	true (−1)	true (−1)
	true (−1)	false (0)	false (0)
	false (0)	true (−1)	false (0)
	false (0)	false (0)	false (0)

The relational operators return a value of −1 (for true) or 0 (for false).
Example:
X = 3
PRINT X = 3 ; X > 4 ; X > = 2 - result is −1 0 −1
The logical operators use two byte 2s compliment numbers and do a full bit by bit operation on these bytes. This means that not only can they be

used to connect relational operators in a condition but they can also be used to set and reset specific bits without affecting the others.
Example:

7 AND 3 = 3	7 — 00000000	00000111
	AND	
	3 — 00000000	00000011
	=	
	3 — 00000000	00000011
7 OR 8 = 15	7 — 00000000	00000111
	OR	
	8 — 00000000	00001000
	=	
	15 — 00000000	00001111

The OR operator is used to set specific bits. To set a particular bit, X, in a variable, Y, OR it with 2 ↑ X (e.g. to set bit 7, Y = Y OR 2 ↑ 7). This sets up the second pair of bytes to contain all 0's except in the bit you specified and when this is ORed with the original number, that bit is set and the others are unaffected. Note that more than one bit can be set at the same time.
Example:
Y = Y OR 2 ↑ 7 + 2 ↑ 3 sets both bits 7 and 3.

To reset specific bits is a bit harder. The AND operator is used with a number which has all its bits set except for the one you wish to reset. Probably the easiest way to produce this number to be ANDed is to use the NOT operator which simply sets all the bits reset, and resets all the bits set. Therefore, to reset bit 7 in Y the expression, Y = Y AND NOT 2 ↑ 7 is used. Again as with the OR operator more than one bit may be reset with the one AND operation.

The AND operator can also be used to check if particular bits are set, eg. to see if bit 7 is set in Y then AND Y with 2 ↑ 7. If bit 7 is set then 2 ↑ 7 will be returned otherwise 0 will be returned. As conditions are taken to be true if the number is non-zero then this can easily be used in an IF statement.
e.g. IF (Y AND 2 ↑ 7) THEN PRINT " BIT 7 IS SET" ELSE PRINT " BIT 7 IS NOT SET"

Numerics are stored as a 4 byte mantissa and 1 byte exponent (see chapter 5) and are operated on in this format, but converted into two byte 2's complement format for comparison.

Possibly the best way to become familiar with the OR, AND and NOT functions is to try out various examples and see what results you obtain.

Character strings can be linked together with the operator "+". They can also be compared using the same comparison operators as used in numerics.

The comparison operators work on the character ASCII codes for each string. Strings are equal if all character codes are equal. The character string first having an ASCII code smaller than the other is said to be less than the other. If strings are the same except that one is longer then the shorter one is considered to be the smaller.
Examples:
"ASM" > "ASB"
"ASMT" < "ASMTQ"
"ALL" < "ZERO"

LINES

BASIC statements can be executed directly from the keyboard or stored in a program. If a statment is typed in preceeded by a line number (0-63999) then the statement is automatically put in the program, sorted in numerical order, otherwise it is executed immediately.
More than one BASIC statement can be on the same line, both for a program or for immediate execution by separating them with a colon (:).
Spaces are optional in BASIC. Extra spaces between keywords, variable names, symbols and constants are ignored and the only time a space is required is if a BASIC keyword follows on from a variable name, these must then have a space between them.
Example:
IF A = B THEN — correct
IFA = B THEN — correct
IFA = BTHEN — incorrect, as BTHEN would be regarded as a variable name

BASIC COMMANDS

AUDIO

- Connect/disconnect cassette output to TV
- AUDIO ON
  AUDIO OFF
- Connecting the cassette to the TV allows you to record sound effects on tape then play them back under program control (see MOTOR) to add special sound effects to programs.
- AUDIO ON .00050 sec.
  AUDIO OFF .00044 sec.

CIRCLE

- Draw a circle on the graphics screen
- CIRCLE ([x],[y]), [r]
  CIRCLE ([x],[y]), [r], [attribute list]

where the [attribute list] is made up of some or all of the following options: [c], [hw], [start], [end], separated by commas.

- This command will draw a circle on the current graphic page (see PMODE, Chapter 2.)

Parameters are:

— x,y : position of the centre of the circle (x=0-255,y=0-191)
— r : radius of circle
— c : colour (0 - 8) optional, default is foreground colour
— hw : height-width ratio : (used for drawing elipses) optional. The width of the circle is always two times the radius you specified. The height-width ratio determines how high the circle is, default is 1
— start, end : starting and ending positions of the circle (0 - 1), position 0 of the circle is 3 o'clock, .25 is 6 o'clock position, etc. Whenever the starting position is greater than the ending position, or when either start or end is omitted, a complete circle is drawn. When the start and end positions are specified the hw option must also be specified.

- CIRCLE (128, 96), 30
  CIRCLE (128,96), 30,, 0.5
  CIRCLE (128,96), 30,, 1.25, .75

- CIRCLE (1,1),1–0.0958 secs
  CIRCLE (1,1),1000–0.1514 secs
  CIRCLE (1,1),10,2,3.5–0.1125 secs
  CIRCLE (1,1), 10, 2, 3.5, .75–0.0812 secs

CLEAR

- Initialize variables, reserve string space and set highest BASIC address
- CLEAR [string space], [address]
- Sets all numeric variables to 0 and string variables to null strings. If the [string space] is specified then that many bytes is reserved for string storage space, default is 200. If the [address] is specified then that is the highest address that BASIC will use, leaving a 'safe' area for machine code routines. Note that if [address] is specified then [string space] must also be specified
- CLEAR
  CLEAR 100
  CLEAR 300,10000

CLOAD

- Load a BASIC program from tape
- CLOAD
  CLOAD ""
  CLOAD "[filename]"
- Will load a program from tape in either token form or ASCII form (see CSAVE). If [filename] is specified the program with that name will be loaded otherwise the first program found is loaded. [filename] must be 8 characters or less.
- CLOAD
  CLOAD "DRAGON 1"
  CLOAD ""

CLOADM

- Load a machine code program from tape
- CLOADM
  CLOADM""
  CLOADM"[filename]"
  CLOADM"", [offset]
  CLOADM"[filename]", [offset]
- This loads a machine code program (or block of memory — see CSAVEM) from tape. If [filename] is specified the file with that name will be loaded otherwise the first file found will be loaded. If the [offset] is specified, this is added to the value of the addresses that were saved, otherwise the original addresses are used.
- CLOADM
  CLOADM "DRAGON M"
  CLOADM "DRAGON M", 1024

CLOSE

- Closes open files or devices
- CLOSE [device-number]

where [device-number] is either #−1 or #−2

- When a cassette data file (#−1) is CLOSEd, if it has been used in output mode, the data remaining in the buffer and an EOF marker is put on the tape; if it has been used as input then the buffer is cleared; either way the buffer is made available for another OPEN command.

There seems to be no effect when closing files for device #−2 (the printer).
CLOSE with no parameter closes all currently open files.
(See OPEN#−1)

- 0.00280 secs.

CLS

- Clear the screen and set background colour
- CLS [colour]
- Clears the screen and if [colour] is specified sets the screen to that colour otherwise green is used by default.
- CLS
  CLS 3
- CLS .00807 secs
  CLS x .00997 secs

COLOR

- Set foreground and background colours on a graphic page.
- COLOR [foreground], [background]
- Set the foreground and/or the background colours (within limits - see Colour Sets) for a graphic page.
  Defaults are : [foreground] - lowest available colour
  [background] - highest available colour
- COLOR 3
  COLOR 3,5
- COLOR x .00225 secs
  COLOR x,y .00412 secs

CONT

- Continue a program
- CONT
- After the BREAK key is pressed or a STOP or END statement is executed, the program can be re-started from the next statement using the CONT command. CONT will not work if any changes have been made to the program (by EDIT or adding lines) or if another command was entered incorrectly and an error message given between the BREAK and CONT. CONT always resumes execution at the next statement after the program was stopped.
- CONT

CSAVE

- Save BASIC programs on tape
- CSAVE
  CSAVE ""
  CSAVE "[filename]"
  CSAVE "",A
  CSAVE "[filename]",A
- Saves a BASIC program on tape either in token format (the internal tokens are saved) or ASCII format (actual words saved) selected by ',A'at the end of the command. The program name can be up to 8 characters (any character except " can be used).

Note: If ASCII format is to be specified then the quotation ("") marks must be used, even if no program name is to be specified.

- CSAVE
  CSAVE "",A
  CSAVE "DRAGON 1"

CSAVEM

- Save a machine language routine on tape.
- CSAVEM "",[start],[end], [entry]
  CSAVEM "[filename]", [start], [end], [entry]
- Blocks of memory are saved on tape. [filename]is the name of the file, [start] is the first address to be saved, [end] is the last address to be saved and [entry] is the first address to be executed when the first EXEC command is given after the program is reloaded.
- CSAVEM "SCROLL", 10000, 11000, 10100

Note: The parameters may be specified in decimal, hexadecimal or octal by following the normal rules for numeric constants.

DATA

- Stores data in your program
- DATA [value], [value], ...
- The DATA statement allows you to keep both numeric and string data in your program. Each piece of data is separated by a comma. If you require a comma in your string then that piece of data must be enclosed in quotation ("") marks. If a piece of data starts with a quotation (") mark then every character (including commas) up to the next quotation mark will be put in the string-variable.
- 10 FOR I = 1 TO 5 : READ X$: PRINT X$: NEXT I
  20 DATA ",,10,",HELLO"DRAGON",10,HELLO,GOODBYE"

Result:
,,10,
HELLO"DRAGON"
10
HELLO
GOODBYE"

DEF FN

- Define numeric function
- DEF FN [name] ([var]) = [expression]
- This sets up a user defined function. [expression] may be any mathematical expression and use any of the program variables. Note that the variable defined in brackets (after the name) can only be used inside the formula and will not affect a variable of the same name outside the definition. The function can then be called in your program like any

other BASIC function. If a function is defined in two places of a program then the last executed definition is used.
Note: DEF FN cannot be executed in immediate mode, only in a program.
Example:

```
 5 Y = 10
10  DEF FNRR(X) = X / 2 + Y
15  PRINT FNRR(7)
```

Result - 13.5

DEFUSR

- Define machine language routine
- DEFUSR[n] = [address]
- Specifies the starting address of a machine language routine (0 - 65535). You can specify up to 10 user machine language routines by specifying [n] as 0 - 9, default is 0.
- 10 DEFUSR = 11000

DEL

- Deletes program lines
- DEL [lines-desc]
- Delete lines specified in [lines-desc]. Values of [lines-desc] are:

[n] — delete line [n]
[−] — delete entire program
[−n] — delete up to and including line [n]
[n−] — delete from line [n] including line [n]
[n1−n2] — delete from line [n1] to line [n2] inclusive

- DEL 10−50

DIM

- Define (dimension) one or more arrays
- DIM [name] ([dim-list]), [name]([dim-list]),...
- Define one or more arrays with the name [name] and size [dim-list]. When a single number is used in [dim-list] that is the upper bound of the array and subscripts are in the range 0 to upper bound inclusive. Multi-dimensional arrays are defined by separating each dimension upper bound by a comma in the [dim-list]. Both constants and variables may be used in [dim-list]
- DIM A(10), B(5,7), C(D), E$(7)

DRAW

- Draw a line on a graphic page.
- DRAW [command string]
- [command string] can be a constant string (enclosed in quotes) or a string variable, or a combination concatenated with '+'.

[command string] may contain any of the following:

COMMANDS:

M— move draw position. Mx, y—position on screen (x = 0 – 255, y = 0 – 191). M + x, + y— move relative to current position. Note that if it is a positive offset the plus sign must be included.
U— move/draw position up. Ux go up x positions
D— move/draw position down. Dx go down x positions
L— move/draw position left. Lx go left x positions
R— move/draw position right. Rx go right x positions
E— move/draw position 45° angle x positions
F— move/draw position 135° angle x positions
G— move/draw position 225° angle x positions
H— move/draw position 315° angle x positions
X— execute a substring and return

MODES:

C— change colour to x
A— tilt everything at an angle. x = 0 – 3 means angle is 0°, 90°, 180°, 270°
S— change the scale of everything. x = 1 – 64 indicates the scale factor in units of 1/4
Example:
x = 2 Scale factor 2/4 or 1/2
x = 8 scale factor 8/4 or 2 (double)

OPTIONS:

B— immediately before any motion command, blanks that command i.e. move but not draw.
N— immediately before any motion command, does not update position i.e. draw but return to original cursor position.

```
•DRAW "BM128,96 ; C8 ; U25 ; R25 ; D25 ; L25
 A$ = "U10 ; L10 ; D10 ; R10"
 DRAW A$
 B$ = "128,96"
 DRAW A$ + "M" + B$
 DRAW "BM128,96 XA$; C8 U10 L10 D10 R10"
```

EDIT

- change program lines
- EDIT [line]
- After typing EDIT and a line number the line is displayed and the cursor placed underneath the line : it is now ready for editing

Commands are:
nC— change n characters
nD— deletes n characters

I — insert new characters
H — deletes rest of lines and waits for new input
L — list current line and continue edit
nSc — searches for the nth occurence of the character 'c'
X — extend line; add new characters to the end of the line
SHIFT ↑ — escape from sub command
n SPACE — move n spaces to the right
n ← — move n spaces to the left
K — deletes rest of line — from current position
nKc — deletes the line up to the nth occurence of the character 'c'

END

- Ends program execution
- END
- Terminates program execution. Program maybe restarted on the next line with CONT. This is optional and, if not included, program execution ends with the last BASIC statement.

EXEC

- Transfer control to machine language program
- EXEC [address]
- Control is passed to a machine code program starting at [address]. if the address if not specified control passes to the address used in the last CLOADM command. When the machine code program executes an RTS command, control is returned to the next BASIC command (if entered directly, to the command level)
- EXEC 10000

FOR

- Create a loop in the program
- FOR [variable] = [n1] TO [n2] ... /NEXT [variable]
  FOR [variable] = [n1] TO [n2] STEP [n3] ... /NEXT [variable]
- Creates a loop which executes the commands between the FOR and the NEXT commands. The variable specified in [variable] is initialized to [n1]. Each time through the loop [n3] (default 1) is added to the [variable] and the statements executed until [variable] equals or surpasses [n2]. When [variable] equals [n2] the statements are executed and control is passed to the statement after the NEXT statements. If [variable] does not equal [n2] (has incremented past [n2]) control is passed directly to the statement following the NEXT statement.

Note:
The loop is always executed once.

```
10 FOR I = 1 TO 5 STEP 2 : X$(I) = "HELLO" + STR$(I) : NEXT I
20 FOR I = 1 TO 5
30 PRINT I, X$(I)
```

40 NEXT I
50 FOR I = 5 TO 1 STEP −3 : PRINT I, X$(I) : NEXT I
Result:
1 HELLO1
2
3 HELLO3
4
5 HELLO5
5 HELLO5
2
- FOR I = 1 TO 10 : NEXT I - 0.001868 secs per loop

GET
- Save a rectangle of graphics screen
- GET ([x1],[y1]) − ([x2],[y2]) , [variable]
  GET ([x1],[y1]) − ([x2],[y2]) , [varable] , G
- Gets a rectangle of the screen specified by the diagonally opposed corners, [x1],[y1] and [x2],[y2] and places it in the array [variable] (see Chapter 2 for a full discussion). The syntax also allows for a 'G' to be added at the end of the command to specify that full graphic detail is to be saved.
- GET (10,10) − (20,20), A
- GET (10,10) − (15,15), A - 0.01808 secs
  GET (10,10) − (30,30), A - 0.03231 secs

GOSUB
- Perform a subroutine
- GOSUB [line-number]
- Control is passed to the BASIC line whose number is specified by [line-number] and execution continues until a RETURN is encountered, then control is passed to the statement following the originating GOSUB.

```
 10 GOSUB 100
 20 PRINT "HELLO";
 30 END
100 PRINT "SAY "
110 RETURN
```

Result:
SAY HELLO
- GOSUB/RETURN - 0.00181 secs

GOTO
- Pass control of program to another line
- GOTO [line-number]
- Control is passed to the BASIC line whose line number is specified by [line-number] and execution continues from there.

```
10 GOTO 40
20 PRINT "THERE"
30 END
40 PRINT "HELLO";
50 GOTO 20
```

Result:
HELLO THERE

- 0.00093 secs

IF/THEN/ELSE

- Test relationships
- IF [condition] THEN [statements **or** line-number]
  IF [condition] GOTO [line-number]
  IF [condition] THEN [statements **or** line-number] ELSE [statements **or** line-number]
  IF [condition] GOTO [line-number] ELSE [statements **or** line-number]
- [condition] can be any numerical or relational expression and is said to be true if it does not equal zero. If [condition] is true then the statements following THEN (up to ELSE or the end of the line) are executed or control is passed to the line having [line-number] after THEN or GOTO.

If [condition] is not true (false, zero) and there is an ELSE, the statements following it are executed or control passed to the line having [line-number] after ELSE.

If [condition] is false and there is no ELSE, control is passed to the next BASIC line.

- A = 27 : B = 16 : X = 11 : A$ = "YES"

IF A = B THEN 200 ELSE300 - Next line executed is 300.
IF X GOTO 1000 - Next line executed is 1000.
IF A$ = "YES" THEN PRINT "OK" ELSE B$ = "NO" : GOTO 20 - OK is printed.
IF A < B THEN A = B : B = 0 : GOTO 300 - Nothing will happen; next line executed is the next line number.

- 0.00274 secs

INPUT

- Enter data from keyboard
- INPUT "[prompt string]" ; [var1], [var2], ...
- When the INPUT command is executed the [prompt string] is displayed (if one has been given) then a question mark and the computer waits for the keyboard input.

The [prompt string] must be a constant in quotes. The question mark is placed directly after the string with no blanks. Note that if [prompt string] is used it must be followed by a semicolon (';'). If no [prompt string] is used, the quote marks ("") are not required.

When multiple variables are to be entered on one line they can either be entered one at a time with an ENTER keystroke after each one or all on one line separated by commas.

• INPUT "TWO NUMBERS PLEASE" ; A, B
INPUT A$
INPUT "YES OR NO" ; ANS$

INPUT#−1

• Enter data from tape
• INPUT#−1 [prompt string] ; [var1], [var2], ...
  INPUT#−1 [var1], [var2], ...
• Accepts data from tape that has been previously recorded using PRINT#−1. Note that if the data on tape is of a different type or format the program will halt with an FM, FD or IO error.
If a prompt string is used it is ignored and has no effect. It can be used as a comment in the program. (see OPEN#−1)
• INPUT#−1 "TAPE DATA", AB$
  INPUT#−1, A, B

LET

• Assign a variable a value.
• LET [var] = [expression]
• The LET keyword is an option when assigning variables values. It is included because many version of BASIC require it and programs from these machines can, at times, be used on the DRAGON without extensive modification.
• LET A = 34 / X
• LET B$ = "DRAGON"
• LET B$ = B$ + "IS HERE"
• 0.00157 secs

LIST

• List program on the screen.
• LIST [line-desc]
• List entire program or lines specified in [line-desc] onto the screen.
Format of [line-desc] is as follows:
n — list line n
−n — list all lines up to and including n
n− — list all lines after n, including n
n1−n2 — list all lines between n1 and n2 inclusive
If no [line-desc] is given then the complete program is listed.
• LIST
LIST −30
LIST 40−70

LLIST

- List program on line printer
- LLIST [line-desc]
- Same as LIST except the listing is done on the printer.
- LLIST
  LLIST 100–

LINE

- Draws a line
  LINE ([x1],[y1]) – ([x2],[y2]), [a]
  LINE ([x1],[y1]) – ([x2],[y2]), [a], [b]
- Draws a line from the starting point [x1],[y1]to the end point [x2], [y2]. If the starting point is omitted the ending point of the last LINE or DRAW command is used or, if there isn't a previous LINE or DRAW command, the line will start at (126, 96).

[a] must be either PSET or PRESET. If PSET is used then the line is drawn in the foreground colour. If PRESET is used the line is drawn in the background colour, that is, the line is erased.

Either B (Box) or BF (Box Filled) can be used as the [b] option. If B is specified a rectangle is drawn using the start and end positions as two diagonally opposed corners. If the BF option is used the rectangle is drawn, then filled in with solid colour.

- LINE (0,0) – (100,100), PSET, B
  LINE – (120,150), PSET
  LINE (0,100) – (100,100), PSET
- LINE .03 secs
  BOX .037 secs
  BOXFILLED 4 secs

LINE INPUT

- Enter data from keyboard
- LINE INPUT "[prompt string]" ; [var]
  LINE INPUT [var]
- The difference between INPUT and LINE INPUT is that LINE INPUT will take the entire line including leading blanks and commas and place it in a string variable. LINE INPUT cannot be used for numerical input and has a maximum length of 255 characters. Only one variable may be used. There is no question mark after the prompt string.
- LINE INPUT "HELLO LINE?" ; ANS$

MOTOR

- Turn the cassette motor on or off
- MOTOR ON
  MOTOR OFF
- Allows the motor of the cassette to be controlled by a program for creating special effects (see AUDIO)
- MOTOR ON 0.5272 secs
  MOTOR OFF 0.0005 secs

NEW

- Clears the current BASIC program from memory. This does not actually erase any of the memory but rather modifies the pointers to the BASIC program so that it cannot be accessed.

ON..GOSUB

- Multibranch to subroutines
- ON [var] GOSUB [line-number1], [line-number2], ...
- This allows multiple GOSUB commands on the one line. Depending on the value of [var] a branch to a subroutine is executed. If [var] is 1, then [line-number1] is used, if [var]is 2, then [line-number2] is used, etc. If [var] is zero or greater than the number of line numbers specified then the statement following the ON-GOSUB statement is executed. Negative values of [var] will cause an error. Values of [var] that are not integers are reduced to integers by removing the fraction.
- ON X GOSUB 100, 200, 300, 400, 500
- 0.00258 secs

ON .. GOTO

- Multi-branches
- ON [var] GOTO [line-number1], [line-number2], ...
- Same as ON .. GOSUB except the branches are to lines not to subroutines.
- ON X GOTO 10, 20, 30, 40, 70
- 0.00258 secs

OPEN

- Opens a data file.
- OPEN "[a]",#—1, [filename]
- Opens a file on tape for either reading or writing. [a] determines whether you can read or write. The legal values of [a] are 'O' and 'I' which stand for Output and Input respectively.

When a file is opened a buffer of 255 bytes is set up in BASIC's work area. If the file was opened for input this will then be filled up with data

from the tape and whenever all the data is INPUT#−1ed from the buffer it will be filled again from the tape automatically. When a file is opened for output and PRINT#−1 statements are executed the data does not immediately get put onto tape, but rather, into this buffer and when the buffer is full or the file is closed the data is transferred onto the tape.
- OPEN "I",#−1, "ADDRESSES"
- 0.00387 secs

PAINT
- Paints a section of a graphics page.
- PAINT ([x],[y])
  PAINT ([x],[y]), [colour]
  PAINT ([x],[y]), [colour], [border]
- Paints a section of a graphics page, starting at position [x], [y], with colour [colour]. If [colour] is not specified the current foreground colour is used. The painting will be contained by a border of colour [border]. Note that if there is any small gap in the border then the painting will 'escape' outside of the border and continue until it is contained by another border or fills the whole screen. If [border] is omitted then the entire screen will be painted, regardless of the values of x and y.
- PAINT (10,10), 3, 1
  PAINT (100, 100)
- Time is approx. 4 secs for half a screen.

PCLEAR
- Reserve memory for graphics
- PCLEAR [n]
- Reserve [n] pages for graphics memory. [n] can be in the range 1-8. The contents of the memory reserved are not affected. This should be done near the start of the BASIC program as there may be strange side-effects if done in the middle.

This effects the amount of memory available for BASIC. For the maximum memory available to BASIC use PCLEAR1.
- PCLEAR 5
- 0.00477 secs

PCLS
- Clears graphic pages
- PCLS [n]
- Clears the current graphics page to colour [n]. If [n] is not specified the current background colour is used.

This should be done whenever PMODE selects a new graphics resolution.
- PCLS
  PLCS 4
- 0.0274 secs

PCOPY

- Copy graphics pages
- PCOPY [n1] TO [n2]
- Copies the graphic page [n1] to the graphic page [n2].
- PCOPY 2 TO 4
- 0.02605 secs for PMODE 1

PLAY

- Play music
- PLAY [command string]
- Play music as specified in [command string]. Commands in the string are:

A-G	notes
1-12	tones
On	Octave n (0-5) default 2
Vn	Volume n (0-31) default 15
Ln	Length of notes (1-255) default 1
Tn	Tempo n (1-255) default 2
Pn	Pause n (1-255)
Xn$	Executes string n$ and returns
# or +	Sharp
–	flat
.	½ as long again

For a more detailed explanation of the PLAY command see Chapter 4.

- PLAY "A ; B ; C ; D ; E #"

PMODE

- Select resolution and graphic page
- PMODE [n1], [n2]
- Select the resolution to be [n1] and the starting graphic page to be [n2]. Defaults are 2 for resolution and the last page is used for start page.
- PMODE, 3
  PMODE 1
  PMODE 1, 3
- 0.00448 secs

POKE

- Fill a memory location with a specified value.
- POKE [address], [val]
- Set the memory location specified by [address] (0 - 32538) to the value specified by [val]. The value 'poked' is to be between 0 and 255 (one byte).
- POKE 10000, 100
- 0.00931 secs

PRESET

- Set to background colour
- PRESET ([x],[y])
- Set a point on the graphic page to the background colour. The point is specified by [x] (0 - 255) and [y] (0 - 191).
- PRESET (10,10)
- 0.00477 secs

PRINT

- Display information on the screen
- PRINT [expression] [separator] [expression] [separator] ...
- Outputs character on the TV screen. When no expression is given, a blank line is left. The [expression] may be any numeric or string expression, including string constants. The legal values of the [separator] are comma ',' , semicolon ';' , or a space ' ' . If a comma is used the output will be in two columns, each 15 characters wide. If the first expression is longer than 15 characters then the second expression is printed on the next line down. If the second is too long it 'wraps around' onto the next line down.

With a semicolon, or a space, strings are printed next to each other and numeric items have a space on either side of them. The semicolon holds the cursor in its last position ready for the next PRINT statement.

Note that a question mark may be used instead of the PRINT keyword.

- PRINT "12345678910"
  A$ = "12345678910"
  PRINT A$
  ? A, B;
  PRINT B$A
- PRINT "12345678910" - 0.00506 secs
  PRINT A$ - 0.00487 secs

PRINT USING

- Formatted output
- PRINT USING [format string] [output list]

This outputs variables in a specified format. [format string] specifies how the data is to be printed and can be either a string constant or string variable.

[output list] is a list of variables to be printed separated by commas (,).
[format string] may contain the following:
'.' - indicates the column in which the decimal point is to be displayed.
'#' - indicates the column to display a digit.
The format creates a field which size should be the same as the number of digits in the number to be printed. If the number to be printed has less

digits than specified it is right justified, ie., it is pushed to the right, up to the decimal point or the end of the field. The remaining columns in the field are filled with blanks. If there are no integer digits in the number, a zero is placed to the left of the decimal point. If the number to be printed has more digits than the specified field a '%' is placed at the start of the number and the complete number is printed.

',' - indicates that there is to be a comma to the left, of every third digit to the left of the decimal point. The comma must be specified between the start of the field and the decimal point.
'**' - placed at the start of a field specifies that all unfilled columns to the left be filled with asterisks.
'$' - indicates that the number is to be preceded by a dollar sign at the start of the field definition.
'$$' - indicates the dollar sign is to be on the immediate left of the number, i.e. it is floating.
'**$' - indicates that the unused columns to the left of the floating dollar sign will contain asterisks.
'+' - placed at the start or end of a field specification will be printed as "+" for positive numbers or "−" for negative numbers in the appropriate place (indicates sign).
'−' - placed at the end of a field specification will be printed "−" for negative numbers and " " for positive numbers (indicates negative sign only).
↑↑↑↑ - indicates that the number is to be printed in exponential form ('scientific notation').
! - indicates that only the first character of the string is to be printed.
%*spaces*% - specifies the length of the string variable to be printed. If the length of the string to be printed is smaller than the length of the specification it is left justified, if it is greater then only the first characters - up to the length of the specification - will be printed.
Any other characters will be printed as they appear.

PRINT USING "#####";66.2	66
PRINT USING "##;66.2	%66
PRINT USING "#.#";66.25	%66.3
PRINT USING "########,";1234567	1,234,567
PRINT USING "**####";66.2	**** 66
PRINT USING "$####.##";18.6735	$ 18.67
PRINT USING "$$####.##";18.6735	$18.67
PRINT USING "**$.###";8.333	*$8.333
PRINT USING "+**###";6.217	****+6
PRINT USING "####.#−";−8124.420	8124.4−
PRINT USING "##.####↑↑↑↑";123456	1.2346E+05
PRINT USING "!";"ARITHMETIC"	A
PRINT USING "% %";"NUMERALS"	NUMERAL
PRINT USING "SCORE######,";SC	SCORE 1,000
PRINT USING "### IS LESS THAN ###";A,B	10 IS LESS THAN 11

PRINT @

- Place output at a specified location
- PRINT @ [expression], [print list]
- [expression] can be any numeric expression between 0 and 511 and specifies where on the screen to start the printing (see Appendix H for locations).

[print list] is the same as for a normal PRINT statement

- PRINT @ 192, "HELLO"
- 0.00740 secs

PRINT#

- Output to other devices
- PRINT#−1, [print list]
  PRINT#−2, [print list]
  PRINT USING #−1, [format string] ; [print list]
  PRINT USING #−2. [format string] ; [print list]
- Has the same function as other PRINT statements except output is directed to: cassette for #−1, printer for #−2.

PSET

- Set a point on the graphic page to a specific colour.
- PSET ([x],[y],[c])
- Set a point on the graphic page to the colour specified by [c]. If [c] is omitted then the colour is set to the foreground colour. The point is specified by [x] (0 - 255) and [y] (0 - 191).
- PSET (1,1,2)
- 0.00694 secs

PUT

- Puts the graphics stored in an array onto the graphic page.
- PUT ([x1],[y2]− [x2],[y2]), [a], [b]
- Puts the graphics stored in array [a] onto the graphic page at location specified by [x1], [y1] (top left corner) and [x2], [y2] (bottom right corner) with the action specified in [b].

Values of [b] can be:
PSET — sets all the points set in the array.
PRESET — resets all the points set in the array.
AND — sets all points that are set both in the array and on the screen, otherwise reset the point. (Sets all points common to both.)
OR — sets all points that are set in either the array or the screen. (Sets all points that are set).
NOT — reverses the screen in the area specified regardless of what is in the array. That is, all points set are reset and all points reset are set.
The array must be the correct size (see Chapter 2).

- PUT (10,10) − (20,20), A, PSET
- 0.01149 secs for a 10x10 array

READ

- Gets the next item from a DATA statement.
- READ [var1], [var2], ...
- Reads the next item of data from a DATA line and places it in [var]. An error results if there is no data to READ. A pointer is kept at the next element to be read (see RESTORE).
- READ A
  FOR X = 1 TO 10 : READ A : NEXT X
- 0.00998 secs

REM

- Remark
- REM
  '
- Allows the use of comments in the program. Everything from the REM to the end of the line is ignored.
- 10 'THIS IS IGNORED
  20 X = 0 : REM INITIALIZE X
- empty -0.00042 secs
100 characters - 0.00485 secs

RENUM

- Renumbers the program lines
- RENUM [newline], [startline], [increment]
- Renumbers all program lines from [startline] to the end of the program. [newline] is the value that the [startline] is renumbered to. All line numbers after [startline] are incremented by the value of [increment]. All line numbers embedded in the program (eg. GOTO 200) are changed accordingly. All parameters are optional and the default value for all parameters is 10.
- RENUM
  RENUM,,5
  RENUM, 100, 100

RESET

- Set a point on the text screen to the background color.
- RESET ([x],[y])
- Sets a point on the text screen to the background color, that is, erases it. The point is specified by [x] (0 - 63) and [y] (0 - 31).
- RESET (0,0)
  RESET (10,10)
- 0.00460 secs

RESTORE

- Allow rereading of data
- RESTORE
- Restores the data pointer to the start of the DATA statements allowing them to be reread.
- RESTORE
- 0.00039 secs

RETURN

- Return from subroutine
- RETURN
- Returns control to the main BASIC program after a subroutine has been executed. Processing is resumed at the statement following the last GOSUB executed. RETURN is the last statement in a subroutine.
- 10 PRINT "THIS IS A SUBROUTINE"
  20 RETURN

RUN

- Start a program
- RUN [line]
- Start the BASIC program executing at [line]. If [line] is omitted then execution starts at the lowest line number. This can also be used inside a program.
- RUN 20

RUN

SCREEN

- Set graphics or text screen and colour set.
- SCREEN [type], [colour-set]
- The [type] parameter sets the type of screen to use either text (0) or graphics (1). The [colour-set] determines the colour set to be used and is either 0 or 1. The colours available depend on the current PMODE setting (for more information see Chapter 2, page 47 and Appendix D). The default settings for both is 0. Note that at least one parameter must be given.
- SCREEN 1
  SCREEN, 1
  SCREEN 1, 0
- 0.00476 secs

SET

- Set a point on the screen.
- SET ([x],[y],[c])

• This sets a point on the text screen. The position of point set is [x] (0 - 63) and [y] (0 -31). The [c] parameter specifies the colour to use (0 - 8), irrespective of the current colour set.
Note that the rest of the points in the character block that contains the points that haven't been specifically SET, are reset to black.
• SET (1,1,7)
  SET (61,25,1)
• 0.00669 secs

SKIPF
• Move past a file on tape
• SKIPF
  SKIPF ""
  SKIPF "[filename]"
• If no name is given at the end of the command, one file is skipped, that is, the tape runs through and stops at the end of the first file encountered. If [filename] is specified the tape will run until the end of the file named. If no file of the name is found the tape will run to the end.
• SKIPF
SKIPF "PROGRAM1"

SOUND
• Generate sound
• SOUND [pitch], [duration]
• [pitch] is a number between 1 and 255 with 1 being the lowest tone. [duration] is a number between 1 and 255. A duration of 16 is approximately 1 second. Note that while the sound is being generated no other processing can be done and the program cannot be stopped with the BREAK key.
• SOUND 100,100

STOP
• Terminate program execution.
• STOP
• The STOP command is the same as the END command except that a "BREAK IN #" message is printed. The CONT command will start execution at the next statement as for END.
• IF ANS$ = "N" THEN STOP ELSE 30

TRON/TROFF
• Turn trace mode on/off.
• TRON
  TROFF

• Trace mode is switched on by TRON and off by TROFF. When a BASIC program is executed in trace mode the line numbers of the program are displayed as they are encountered. The numbers are enclosed in square brackets ('[' and ']').
• TRON
  TROFF
• TRON - 0.00033 secs
  TROFF - 0.00037 secs

BASIC FUNCTIONS

ABS

• Absolute value
• ABS ([argument])
• Returns the absolute value, ie. regardless of + or – signs.
• PRINT ABS(3 –2 * B + 7)
• 0.00230 secs

ASC

• ASCII code
• ASC ([string])
Returns the ASCII code of the first character in the [string] argument.
• 10 AS = ASC ("AND")
  20 PRINT AS
• 0.00267secs

ATN

• Arctangent
• ATN ([argument])
• Returns the arctangent (inverse tangent) of the [argument] in radians.
• PRINT "ANGLE : " ; ATN(R3)
• 0.00622 secs for 0
  0.05562 secs for 100

CHR$

• Character conversion
• CHR$ ([argument])
• Takes the [argument] as an ASCII code and returns the character equivalent (see Appendix E for codes). The argument must be between 0 and 255.
• A$ = CHR$(129)
• 0.00287 secs

COS

- Cosine
- COS ([argument])
- Returns the cosine of the [argument], which is assumed to be in radians.
- CS = COS(X)
- 0.02856 secs

EOF

- End of file
- EOF ([file-number])
- Indicates whether the file specified has more data in it or not. If an INPUT is given when there is no data in the file an error occurs.
- IF EOF(−1) THEN 150 ELSE INPUT#−1 ; A, B$
- 0.00292 secs

EXP

- Natural exponential
- EXP ([argument])
- Raise **e** (natural logarithm) to the power [argument]. Inverse of LOG
- A = EXP(2) + B
- 0.00547 secs for 0
  0.03023 secs for 100

FIX

- Truncate
- FIX ([argument])
- Truncates (removes all digits to the right of the decimal point).
- PRINT FIX (7.75)
- 0.00275 secs

HEX$

- Converts to hexadecimal
- HEX$ ([argument])
- Returns a string containing hexadecimal digits 0 — 9 and A — F which is the equivalent to the decimal [argument] (0 — 65535).
- PRINT HEX$(15), HEX$(73)
- 0.00337 secs

INKEY$

- Character input from keyboard.
- INKEY$
- This returns the last key pressed that has not been INPUT. If no key has been pressed since the last INPUT, LINE INPUT or INKEY$ a null string is returned (ie. the keyboard has a one character buffer).

- ANS$ = INKEY$
- 0.00167 secs

INSTR

- String search
- INSTR ([argument], [string1], [string2])
- Searches [string1] for [string2]. The search starts at the character number, [argument] and returns either the starting position of [string2] or 0 if [string2] is not found.
- IF INSTR (1, "NYny", ANS$) = 0 THEN 30
- 0.00358 secs

INT

- Convert to integer
- INT ([argument])
- Rounds [argument] downwards. Therefore if [argument] is positive the function is the same as FIX.
- A = INT(B / 2.3)
- 0.00340 secs

JOYSTCK

- Find position of joystick
- JOYSTCK ([argument])
- Returns the current horizontal or vertical position of either the left or the right joystick according to [argument]. Values of [argument] are:

0 — horizontal left joystick
1 — vertical left joystick
2 — horizontal right joystick
3 — vertical right joystick

- LX = JOYSTK (0)
- 0.00443 secs

LEFT$

- Left part of string
- LEFT$ ([string],[argument])
- Returns a string which contains the left characters of [string]. The number of characters returned is specified by [argument].
- PRINT LEFT$ ("WILL NOT BE PRINTED", 4)
- 0.00498 secs for 5 characters

LEN

- Length of string

• LEN ([string])
• Returns the number of characters in [string] including characters that are not displayed on the screen (ie. control characters put there either by the system or by the CHR$ function).
• PRINT LEN ("FOUR")
• 0.00285 secs

LOG

• Natural logarithm
• LOG ([argument])
• Returns the natural logarithm of [argument] which must be positive.
• A = LOG (X / 2) + LOG (Y)
• 0.02651 secs

MEM

• Free memory
• MEM
• Returns the amount of memory that is not being used by the system (ie., available for programs and data). MEM does not include the memory needed for the screen and graphics pages etc.
• PRINT MEM
• 0.00159 secs

MID$

• Middle of string
• MID$ ([string], [argument1], [argument2])
• This returns a substring which is in the middle of [string]. [argument1] specifies which character to start at and [argument2] specifies how many characters are to be returned. If [argument2] is omitted, all the characters from [argument1] to the end, are returned. Note that this can be used the other way to replace characters in the middle of a string. The parameters have the same function when it is used this way, except when [argument2] is omitted the number of characters assigned is the length of the string replacing the original string.
• PRINT MID$ ("THIS WILL NOT BE PRINTED!", 1, 4)
A$ = "I AM VERY HAPPY" : MID$(A$, 6, 4) = "NOT " : PRINT A$
Results—THIS
I AM NOT HAPPY
• 0.00683 secs for 3 characters.

PEEK

• Returns contents stored in memory
• PEEK ([address])
• Returns the current value of memory location [address] (0 — 65535).
• PRINT PEEK (15000)
• 0.00292 secs

POINT

- Check for dot on text screen.
- POINT ([x], [y])
- Test a position on the text screen. If the position is a text character, −1 is returned. If there is nothing there, 0 is returned, otherwise the colour (1 — 8) of the dot is returned. [x] is the horizontal position (0 — 63) and [y] is the vertical position (0 — 31).
- IF POINT (X,Y) = C THEN 200
- 0.00509 secs

POS

- Current cursor position
- POS ([argument])
- Returns the current horizontal position of the cursor. Values of [argument] are 0 for screen cursor or −2 for printer head.
- IF POS (0) = 31 THEN PRINT ELSE PRINT " "
- 0.00469 secs

PPOINT

- Check for dot on graphic screen
- PPOINT ([x], [y])
- Checks the position on a graphic screen as specified by [x] and [y] and returns 0 if cell is off and its colour (1 — 8) if it is on.
- IF PPOINT < > 0 THEN 20
- 0.00469 secs

RIGHT$

- Right part of string
- RIGHT$ ([string], [argument])
- Returns a substring which contains the right portion of [string]. The number of characters in the returned string is specified by [argument].
- B$ = "HELLO"
PRINT RIGHT$ (B$,3)
Result — LLO
- 0.00472 secs for 2 characters
0.00751 secs for 20 characters

RND

- Random numbers
- RND ([argument])
- Returns a random integer between 1 and [argument]. If [argument] is 0 then a real number between 0 and 1 is returned.
- B = A (RND (10))
- 0.01149 secs for RND(1)

SGN

- Sign of argument
- SGN (argument])
- Returns the sign of [argument]. If [argument] is negative, −1 is returned. If [argument] is positive, 1 is returned, otherwise [argument] is 0, in which case 0 is returned.
- IF SGN (A) = −1 THEN PRINT "NEGATIVE"
- 0.00269 secs

SIN

- Sine value
- SIN ([argument])
- Returns the sine of [argument]. It assumes that [argument] is in radians.
- PRINT X, "SINE = ";SIN (X)
- 0.00588 secs for 0
  0.03374 secs for 2000

STRING$

- String building
- STRING$ ([argument1], [argument2] **or** [string])
- Makes a string of length [argument1] which contains either the character with the code [argument2] or the first character of [string].
- PRINT STRING$ (10, "AS")

Result — "AAAAAAAAAA"
PRINT STRING$ (10, 45)
Result — "EEEEEEEEEE"

- 0.00423 secs for 1 character
  0.00371 secs for 0 character
  0.00847 secs for 100 characters

STR$

- Numeric to string conversion
- STR$ ([argument])
- Converts a numeric expression, [argument], to a string of digits (0 — 9). Note that the minimum length of the string returned is 2 as the first character of the string is a blank (space).
- PRINT LEFT$ (STR$ (1 / 3), 4)

Result — 0.33

- 0.00292 secs for 0
  0.00904 secs for 50

SQR

- Square root.
- SQR ([argument])

• Returns the square root ($\sqrt[2]{}$) of [argument]. If [argument] is negative then the program halts with an error.
• PRINT SQR (16)
• 0.00245 secs for 0
0.06150 secs for 1,000,000

TAN

• Tangent of argument
• TAN ([argument])
• Returns the tangent of [argument]. It assumes that [argument] is in radians.
• X = TAN (Y / 2)
• 0.02824 secs for 0
0.05921 secs for 10,000

TIMER

• Set or return time
• TIMER
• TIMER acts as a variable in that you can both get its value and assign it a value but it is continuously being incremented (approximately 50 times a second).
The maximum value of TIMER is 65535 and it is reset to 0 if this value is reached.
• TIMER = 0
PRINT TIMER
• 0.00185 secs

USR

• Call user defined routine.
• USR n ([argument])
• Calls a machine language routine that was defined earlier in the program using DEFUSR. For details of machine language routines and the argument see Chapter 4.
• X = USR (Y)

VAL

• String to number conversion
• VAL ([string])
• Returns the numeric equivalent of the digits (0 — 9) in [string]. If [string] contains non-digit characters then only digits to the left of the first non-digit character are converted; if there are no digits before the non-digit character then 0 is returned.
Note that hexadecimal numbers can be converted also.
• B = VAL ("12345")
PRINT VAL ("&HFF")

• 0.00337 secs for 1
0.00875 secs for 120,000

VARPTR

• Address of variable
• VARPTR ([argument])
• This gives the head address where the variable specified by [argument] is located. To find the head address of array variables, specific elements of the array must be passed, e.g. B = VARPTR (A (0)). When one address is known the others can be calculated as each consists of 5 bytes. For details of how variables are stored see Chapter 4.
• B = VAPPTR (A)
• 0.00223 secs

ERRORS IN BASIC

We have found one problem when executing BASIC programs and this is in floating point addition. The error is that if a number is the result of an addition it does not always exactly equal the number displayed.
e.g. 53.74 does not equal 51 + 2.74

This can be demonstrated by the following program:

```
10 X = 53.74 : Y = 51 + 2.74
20 PRINT X, Y
30 IF X = Y THEN PRINT "RIGHT" ELSE PRINT "WRONG"
```

The problem is caused by the last byte of the number (see section on how numbers are stored) being rounded by the addition process and thus there seems to be no set pattern to how the decimal representation is affected (whether the above program, for different numbers, produces RIGHT or WRONG). One way to overcome the problem is to convert the numbers to strings; using STR$, and comparing these as it seems that BASIC converts them into strings correctly.

For example, the above program will work correctly if an extra line is added and line 30 changed. They should read.

```
15 X$ = STR$ (X) : Y$ = STR$ (Y)
30 IF X$ = Y$ THEN PRINT "RIGHT" ELSE PRINT "WRONG"
```

CHAPTER 2

GRAPHICS

Probably the most impressive and powerful feature of the DRAGON is unfortunately also its most confusing; its graphics.

Powerful because of the many BASIC statements which can do just about anything you want to on the high resolution screens but confusing because of the multitude of modes the screen can be set in and the various commands needed to set up these modes.

All these modes and commands are covered later in the chapter, but let me give you a brief, simple (if that's possible) rundown on how the DRAGON handles its graphics.

Basically there are two different things the screen can display; text (normal writing etc.) and graphics (more on this later). The text screen is the old familiar standard screen which you see when you switch most computers on, ie. letters, numbers and the other symbols which also appear on the keyboard. On the DRAGON this is green with a black border and black writing.

The graphics are a little more complicated (most of this chapter is dedicated to it) but basically consists of lines, dots, circles, pictures, etc.

On the DRAGON, high-resolution graphics and text cannot be mixed on the screen at the same time but rather the text screen is displayed unless a program specifies otherwise and even then the text screen will automatically be displayed whenever BASIC references it (e.g. with a PRINT, INPUT, error message or when a program finishes).

On the other hand anything can be put on any particular graphic screen without effecting any of the others or what is being displayed (unless that screen is currently being displayed) at any time. This allows many things to be done 'behind the user's back' on the graphics screen, for example, while he is busy with the text screen, etc.

Not only can the program be setting up pictures on a high resolution screen while the user sees a text screen but also while the user is looking at other high resolution screens. This means that the user may not see the pictures while they are being drawn but instead sees the finished product. Also several high resolution screens can be drawn each one only slightly different. When these are changed at high speed it will appear as if the objects on the screen are moving.

PIXELS AND RESOLUTION

In computer graphics (similar to photographs and printed pictures) the different shapes are made up by many small dots. Each of these dots can be made to be one of several colours and when seen with the other dots around,it creates a picture. These are called picture elements or 'pixels' for short. It is the number of these pixels which control the resolution. Resolution is a measure of the 'quality' of the picture. The higher the resolution (the more pixels),the better the quality of the picture (e.g. photographs have higher resolution than newspaper print which has higher resolution than most computers).

Obviously the higher the resolution, for a given number of colours, the more memory needed to store the information. so there must be a trade-off between the resolution and the amount of memory to be used or the number of colours on the screen. There is also a trade-off between speed and resolution as the more pixels there are, the longer it will take to change them all.

MODES

When the BASIC interpreter was written for the DRAGON the designers decided to implement 1 semigraphic mode and 5 high resolution modes. What they didn't tell you is that the VDG (Video Display Generator) chip that they used is capable of handling 14 different modes; 5 semigraphic and 8 true graphic plus the standard text mode! However, most of these extra modes are not really useful (which is probably why they didn't bother to implement them).

TEXT

The text mode is the old standard that you use for most of your programming. This is the mode you use to type in, run and edit your programs as well as INPUT, PRINT, etc. from inside your BASIC programs. The text mode also incorporates semigraphic 4 as shown below.

SEMIGRAPHIC

Semigrahic modes are so called as each character block is divided into a number of elements (pixels). The number of elements per character block is used to name the mode, i.e. Semigraphic 4 has four elements per character block, Semigraphic 8 has eight elements per character block, etc.

Semigraphic 4 is not really a seperate mode as it is available at the same time as the text mode and is the only semigraphic mode implemented by BASIC.

The other semigraphic modes use the same area of memory as the text mode so that when using these modes the text screen is not preserved.

However information can be put onto the text screen while the graphics screen is being displayed by using POKE. Using the POKE to put information on the text screen is quite simple as the following program demonstrates.

```
10 CLS
20 A$ = "THIS IS PRINTED OUT"
30 FOR I = 1 TO LEN (A$)
40 A = ASC (MID $ (A$,I,1))
50 IF A < 33 or A > 128 THEN A = 96
60 IF A < 64 THEN A = A + 64
70 POKE 1151 + I, A
80 NEXT I
```

Lines 50 & 60 ensure that no inverse, control or graphic characters are printed. Remove these lines if these characters are desired.

GRAPHIC

The true graphic modes are of much higher resolution and are based on dot graphics. The graphic modes implemented by BASIC are the higher resolution graphic modes of the VDG and have very powerful BASIC commands such as LINE, CIRCLE, etc. as well as the low level PSET and PRESET dot graphic commands.

A table comparing the different modes and their attributes is given below. A more detailed description as well as how they are stored in memory and how to set the screen to these modes is given at the end of the chapter.

The graphic modes which are not directly implemented by BASIC are probably not as useful or practical as those that are. These 'non-mode' modes can be set up by a series of PEEKs and POKEs and are cumbersome to set up and use.

Possible applications for all the modes are given below:

Semigraphic 4 — for crude figures and solid blocks of colour, where multiple colours, speed and the ability to mix in text is important.

Semigraphic 6-24 — for higher resolution (in the vertical axis); could be good for accurate bar charts but can be quite wasteful on the space it uses.

Graphics 7-9 — where the amount of memory used by each screen is of paramount importance, e.g. when the program is very large and/or many pages of graphics are used.

Graphics 10,11 — when resolution has to be reasonable but time and the amount of memory used is still important.
Graphics 12,13— probably the most useful mode as resolution is quite good and speed and memory size is still acceptable.
Graphics 14 — for very high resolution graph plotting such as cos, sin and complex 3-D graphs; could also be used in games where speed and memory size are not important; limited however in that only two colours are available.

MODE	RESOLUTION		IMPLEMENTED IN BASIC	NUMBER OF COLOURS PER SCREEN	NUMBER OF BYTES PER SCREEN
	X	Y			
1. Alphanumeric	32	16	YES	2	512 (0.5K)
2. Semigraphic 4	64	32	YES	8	512 (0.5K)
3. Semigraphic 6	64	48	NO	4	512 (0.5K)
4. Semigraphic 8	64	64	NO	8	2048 (2K)
5. Semigraphic 12	64	96	NO	8	3072 (3K)
6. Semigraphic 24	64	192	NO	8	6144 (6K)
7. Graphic	64	64	NO	4	1024 (1K)
8. Graphic	128	64	NO	2	1024 (1K)
9. Graphic	128	64	NO	4	2048 (2K)
10. Graphic	128	96	YES	2	1536 (1.5K)
11. Graphic	128	96	YES	4	3072 (3K)
12. Graphic	128	192	YES	2	3072 (3K)
13. Graphic	128	192	YES	4	6144 (6K)
14. Graphic	256	192	YES	2	6144 (6K)

VIDEO MEMORY

Video memory is the area of RAM used for storing the information to display on the screen.

The area is from 1024 (&H400) upwards. The minimum size for this area in BASIC is 2048 (2K) bytes (enough for the text screen and one graphic page) and can be expanded up to 12800 (12.5K) bytes by using the PCLEAR command. This area can be shrunk down to 512 (0.5K) bytes and expanded up to the top of RAM by setting the Start of BASIC pointer and the Start of Free Memory pointer before loading the program. These

pointers are located at 25 (&H19), 26 (&H1A)and 31 (&H1F), 32 (&H20). To reduce this area to 0.5K bytes these pointers must be set to 1536 (&H600) by the following:
POKE 25, 6
POKE 31, 6

SCREENS AND PAGES

The video memory area is further divided into two sections; the text screen section and the graphics section. The graphics section is again divided this time into 8 pages, each 1536 (1.5K) bytes.

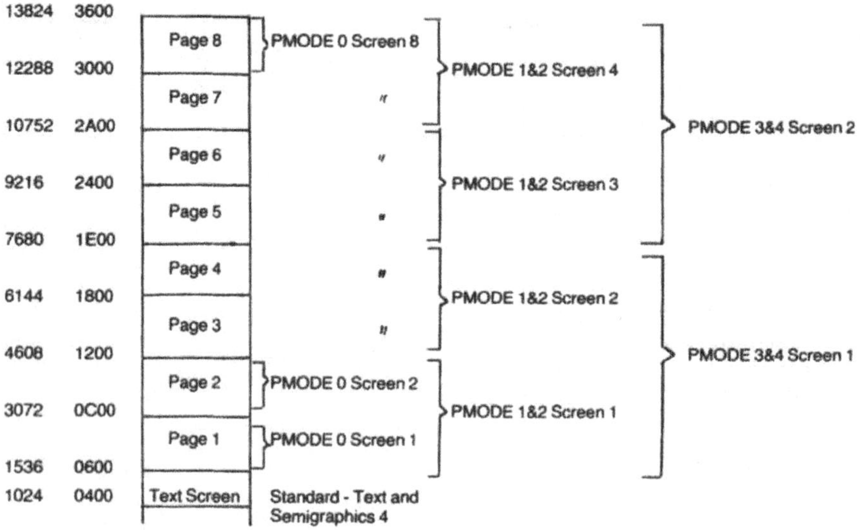

Video Memory

The above diagram shows how the video memory is divided up into pages and screens for the different modes.

PAGE SWAPPING

Apart from having all these different modes, the VDG also has the ability to have the screen displaying the contents of any section of memory. This is limited to a certain number of pages (depending on the resolution) in BASIC but by following the instructions below (setting up addresses &HFFC6 to &HFFD3) or the program Listing 1 the screen can display any section of memory you want to.
Listing 2 demonstrates this by cycling through the entire memory.

LISTING 1

This routine allows easy setting of the start of display area for initialization prior to doing graphics work. Before using this program set the variable S to the address to start, the bottom 9 bits of this address are ignored as addresses can only be multiples of 512.

```
100 S = INT(S / 512)
110 FOR I = &HFFC6 TO &HFFD2 STEP 2
120 R = S – INT (S / 2) * 2 : S = INT (S / 2)
130 POKE I + R, 0
140 NEXT I
```

LISTING 2

```
1  I=0:GOSUB100
2  GOTO2
5  PRINT"PRESS ANY KEY TO MOVE ONTO THE  NEXT BLOCK "
10  FORI=2TO128
20  GOSUB100
30  A$=INKEY$:IFA$=""THEN30
40  NEXTI
50  FORI=0TO2
60  A$=INKEY$:IFA$=""THEN60
70  GOSUB100
80  NEXTI
90  END
100  '** SET UP START OF SCREEN
105  PRINT "UP TO"HEX$(I*512)
106  A$=INKEY$:IFA$=""THEN106
110  S=I/2
120  FORK=&HFFC6 TO &HFFD2 STEP2
130  P=S-INT(S/2)*2:S=INT(S/2)
140  POKE K+P,0
150  NEXTK
160  RETURN
```

There is a 7-bit register in the VDG which controls the start address of the screen. The number in this register is multiplied by 512 to give the actual starting address.

To set this register there are 14 different memory locations, two for each bit.

The relationship between the locations and the register is shown below.

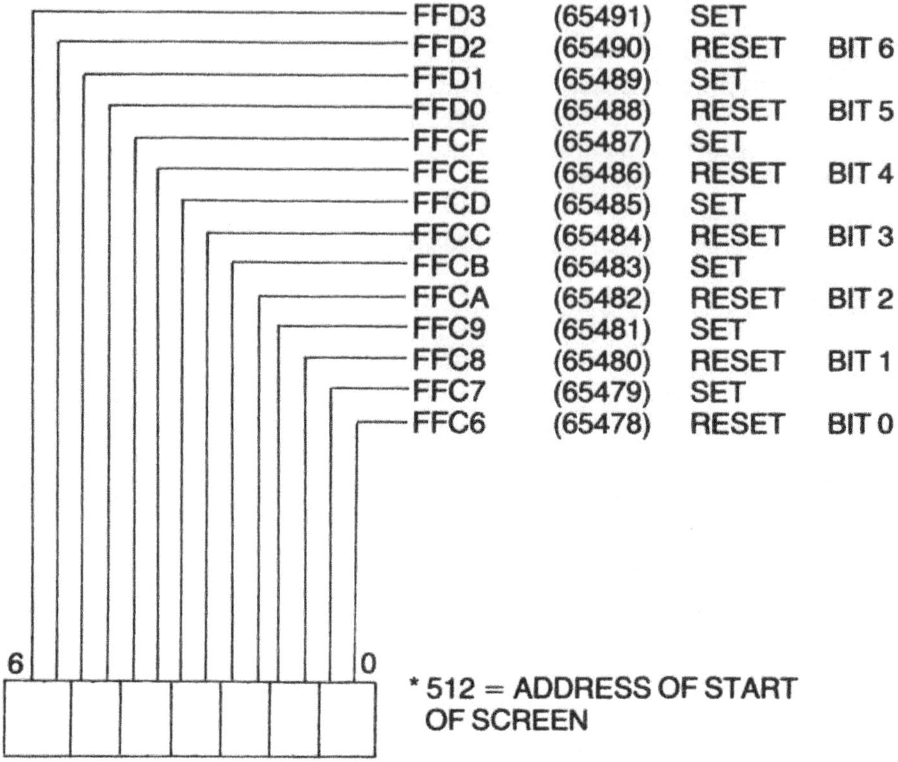

Either a 1 or 0 may be POKEd into the above locations to achieve the appropriate setting or resetting of the bit according to the location. For clarity it is best to use POKE [address], 0 when resetting the bit and POKE [address], 1 when setting the bit.

In BASIC this can be achieved with the PMODE command but only over a limited range of memory. Using this feature can greatly speed up programs which need fast, repetative movement on screen. You can set up in advance slightly different pictures in different areas of memory and cycle throught them rapidly to create the effect of movement.

The rest of this chapter looks at each BASIC graphic command in detail and finishes with a summary of the modes and how to select them.

LOW RESOLUTION (SEMI) GRAPHICS

Unfortunately this is the only resolution in which you can mix graphics and text freely and have all 8 colours on the screen at once. Unfortunate because the resolution is too low (64x32) for any serious picture or games graphics, and even lower (32x16) if you are not using a black background (see SET/RESET). Because of these limitiations it is only suitable for work such as bar charts, crude block figures, etc. The only real advantages of this resolution are that text can be intermingled with the graphics and it is simple and therefore can be fast.

CLS

This command is used to set the entire screen to a particular colour. Note that it does not make this colour the background colour but rather sets all the colour bits to the particular colour and sets all the on/off bits on. When text is put on screen after a CLS [n], wherever the text appears, it is the familiar black on green.

The two exceptions to this are: a CLS without any parameter — this reverts to the standard black on green — and a CLS 0 simply causes all the on/off bits to be off (ie. 0).

SET/RESET

The SET command sets one element to a specified colour. However, there are some surprises. Because the semigraphic 4 mode (standard) has each byte containing four elements, only two colours can exist in the same block (the size of a character) and that is black (i.e. the on/off bit's off) and the color specified in the color bits (i.e. the on/off bit's on). Therefore, when one individual element is turned on the others are turned off. If you are not using a black background you get a big black block with a quarter of it the colour you specified. If any other SETs are done in this block the old one will change to the new one's colour.

The easiest way (but not necessarily the best) to overcome this problem is to only turn the complete block on and off but this reduces the resolution dramatically (to 32x16).

The RESET command simply sets the on/off bits so that that particular element is turned off.

GRAPHICS USING STRINGS

Another way of producing graphics in all the semigraphics modes is to use strings and PRINT them on the screen. By using the CHR$ function with codes greater than 128 (see table below) and adding these together to form strings, pictures can be built up.

GRAPHICS CHARACTERS FOR SEMIGRAPHICS 4

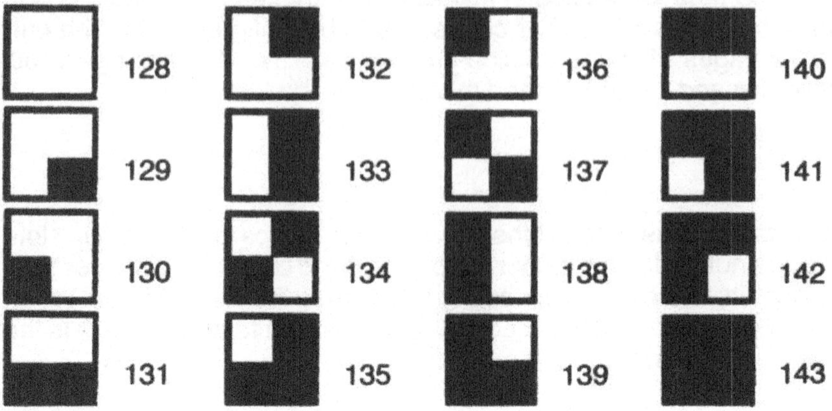

The filled in elements represent those that have their on/off bit set to 1 (i.e. a colour); the other elements have their on/off bits set to 0 (i.e. black).

The above codes represent the filled in elements being green. For different colours add the numbers shown below.
+16 — yellow
+32 — blue
+48 — red
+64 — buff
+80 — cyon
+96 — magenta
+112 — orange
Example:

CHR$ (131)		green
CHR$ (131 + 80)		cyan
CHR$ (142 + 32)		blue

The advantages of using strings to produce graphics is the speed and comparative ease of production and manipulation of shapes (using string handlers such as LEFT$, MID$, etc.). To give some idea of the time saved by using strings, take a shape with 10 characters in it, and in such a way that one PRINT will do all ten. The PRINT statement takes approximately 0.00487 seconds to execute. Each SET statement takes approximately 0.00669 seconds therefore between 10 and 40 SETs (each character can set up to 4 elements) takes between 0.0669 and 0.2676 seconds!

Note that when a PRINT statement is executed, no matter what mode the screen has been set to, it will revert to the standard black on green alpha/sémigraphic 4 mode. Strings can still be used in other modes by doing all the PRINTing on the standard screen before setting the screen to a different mode.

Note also that for different modes the CHR$ function will produce characters (see byte mapping for the various modes at the end of this chapter).

SET/RESET VERSUS STRINGS

Here are two programs to demonstrate the speed advantage of strings, using the old favorite, INVADERS.

Version 1

```
10 A1$=CHR$(128)+CHR$(133)+CHR$(138)+CHR$(128)
20 B1$=CHR$(128)+CHR$(142)+CHR$(141)+CHR$(128)
30 A$=A1$:B$=B1$
40 FORI=1TO5
50 A$=A$+A1$:B$=B$+B1$
60 NEXT
70 CLS0
80 FORI=64TO72
90 PRINT@I,A$;:PRINT@I+32,B$:
100 FORJ=1TO60:NEXT
110 NEXT
120 FORI=71TO65 STEP -1
130 PRINT@I,A$;:PRINT@I+32,B$:
140 FORJ=1TO60:NEXT
150 NEXT
160 GOTn 80
```

Version 2

```
10 CLS
20 FORJ=1TO14:GOSUB50:NEXTJ
30 FORJ=13TO2STEP-1:GOSUB50:NEXTJ
40 GOTO20
50 FORI=1TO48 STEP8
60 RESET(J+I-1,4):RESET(J+I-1,5):RESET(J+1-1,6):
   RESET(J+I-1,7)
70 RESET(J+I,4):RESET(J+I,5)
80 SET(J+I+1,4,0):SET(J+I+1,5,0):SET(J+I+2,4,0):
   SET(J+I+2,5,0)
90 SET(J+I,6,0):SET(J+I,7,0):SET(J+I+1,6,0):
   SET(J+I+2,6,0)
100 RESET(J+I+1,7):RESET(J+I+2,7)
110 SET(J+I+3,6,0):SET(J+I+3,7,0)
120 RESET(J+I+3,4):RESET(J+I+3,5):RESET(J+I+4,6):
   RESET(J+I+4,7)
```

```
130 NEXTI
140 RETURN
```

Obviously neither of these would be used for a serious INVADERS program but it demonstrates the speed which can be acheived using strings.

Note also the ease with which indivual invaders can be removed from strings – simply use the MID$ function to change the middle of the string.

HIGH RESOLUTION GRAPHICS

Altogether there are 15 BASIC commands which work on the hi-res graphic modes. 6 of these are for initializing and manipulating complete screens, 3 for dot graphics and 6 high level graphics commands.

INITIALIZING COMMANDS

SCREEN

The SCREEN command sets the display to either text or the current graphics page as well as selecting the colour set to use. The format of SCREEN is:

SCREEN [type],[colour-set]

Where [type] is 0 for text and 1 for current graphics and [colour-set] is either 1 or 0. The colours available for each colour set depends on the current mode (see below for colours available). The SCREEN command can be used anywhere in a BASIC program but the screen is automatically set to text and color set 0 whenever BASIC has text to display, e.g. PRINT, INPUT, errors, etc.

PCLEAR

The PCLEAR command is used to reserve up to 8 pages of graphic memory. The memory immediately after the graphics pages reserved is used for your BASIC program. For this reason if PCLEAR is to be used it should be close to the beginning, otherwise there may be strange results. There are four pages of graphics reserved when BASIC is initialized. Each page is 1536 bytes long. PCLEAR is used to either increase the number of graphic pages allowing more to be 'flipped through', or to decrease the number of graphic pages leaving more RAM space for your BASIC programs.

PMODE

The PMODE command is used to change the current resolution and starting page of the display. Only modes 10 through 14, and pages 1 to 8, can be selected by PMODE. For imformation about setting other modes and pages see the end of the chapter. PMODE can be used at any time to change the resolution of the screen (note that the SCREEN command must be given to actually see the current page). Below is a table which shows the colours that are available for the various page and colour-set combinations.

PMODE #	COLOUR-SET	COLOURS AVAILABLE
4	0	BLACK/GREEN
	1	BLACK/BUFF
3	0	GREEN/YELLOW/BLUE/RED
	1	BUFF/CYAN/MAGENTA/ORANGE
2	0	BLACK/GREEN
	1	BLACK/BUFF
1	0	GREEN/YELLOW/BLUE/RED
	1	BUFF/CYAN/MAGENTA/ORANGE
0	0	BLACK/GREEN
	1	BLACK/BUFF

PMODE is also used to set the starting mode of the screen display so it can be used to 'flip through' pages of graphics giving a movement effect.

Below is a table showing how many pages are needed for each mode and therefore how many different screens can be stored simultaneously.

MODE	Pages/Screen	# of Screens
4	4	2
3	3	2
2	2	4
1	2	4
0	1	8

Note that if PMODE is used to change resolution or starting pages, even though you may already be in graphics display mode the SCREEN command selecting graphics display mode must be given again as this initializes the variables needed by BASIC to work on the screen. If the SCREEN command is not given after a PMODE strange things will happen to the screen and to how it is accessed.

PCOPY

The PCOPY command is used for copying one graphics page onto another. This allows multiple pages of the same picture or multiple pictures on the same screen by copying a page into the page above it then a high resolution mode is used to display the page.

PCLS

The PCLS command clears the current graphic screen to the specified colour. If the specified colour is not in the current colour set or the colour has not been specified then the current background colour is used. Note that the entire screen is cleared, which may contain more than one page.

COLOR

The COLOR command allows the background and foreground colours to be set. The border (in graphics) is either green or buff and if we set the background to this colour the border disappears. The foreground colour is used as the default colour in other graphic commands.

PRODUCING GRAPHICS

PSET AND PRESET

So much for initializing the screen, now to actually put something on it. The simplest way to produce something on the screen is to use PSET and PRESET. As you may have guessed they are the same as SET and RESET except they work on the graphics screen. Instead of having only 64x32 addressable points on the screen you have 256x192 on the highest resolution and 128x96 on the lowest resolution. It does not matter what resolution is set, the co-ordinates are always 0 — 255 on the horizontal axis and 0 — 191 on the vertical axis. The difference between the resolutions is the size of the points that can be turned on and off. In the lower resolutions there will be more than one co-ordinate that refers to the same point on the screen.

The PSET command is useful for drawing curves such as SIN etc. as the program below shows.

```
 10 PMODE 0, 1
 20 PCLS
 30 SCREEN 1, 1
 40 I = 0
 50 SS = SIN (I)
 60 CS = INT (SS * 80) + 96
 70 PSET (I * 20 - 0, CS)
 80 I = I + 0.01
 90 IF I  <  12.7 THEN 50
100 GOTO 100
```

Try this program changing the resolution of the graphics in line 10. See how the curve stays the same but it becomes smoother as the resolution gets higher.

PPOINT

The other low level graphic command is PPOINT which simply samples a particular pixel and returns the colour the pixel is set to.

HIGH LEVEL

So far we have discussed dot graphics which is OK for curve plotting and simple pictures, etc. but why spend useful time on something that is already done for you?

The BASIC high level commands LINE, CIRCLE and DRAW produce shapes for you without all the complex functions, loops, data, etc. (for examples of the use of these commands see the chapter on handy routines).

LINE

The LINE command not only draws lines, boxes and filled in boxes but also erases lines, boxes and filled in boxes. The format of the LINE commmand is
LINE ([x1],[y1]) – ([x2],[y2]), [fn1], [fn2]

Execution of LINE produces a line that runs from the first co-ordinates through to the second co-ordinates. The colour of the line drawn depends on [fn1]. This is either PSET or PRESET (sound familiar?). If PSET is specified then the line is drawn in the the current foreground colour (set with the COLOR command) and if PRESET is specified the current background colour is used, effectively erasing a line.

[fn2] is an optional function and can be either B or BF, specifying Box or Box Filled. When this option is used a box (rectangle) is drawn with its diagonally opposite corners on the two co-ordinates specified. If the B option is used the box is a line, one graphic element wide, if the BF option is used the box is a solid colour.

CIRCLE

The CIRCLE command, like the LINE command, does more than draw circles; it also draws arcs and elipses. To draw a plain circle the format is:
CIRCLE ([x],[y]), [r], [c]

Were [x] and [y] are the co-ordinates (same as PSET) of the centre of the circle and [r] is the radius. The legal values of [x] are 0 — 255and [y] are 0 — 191.

The radius is specified by [r], [r] can have any value. Any part of the circle that happens to go outside the screen area is ignored. The [c] parameter specifies the colour that the circle is drawn in. If [c] is omitted the current foreground colour is used and if [c] is set to the background colour the circle is effectively erased.

To make the circle an elipse there is an option which allows you to change the height/width ratio. This option immediately follows the colour option. If you are using the H/W parameters but not the colour option, a comma must still be used (e.g. CIRCLE (10,10),10,,3 signifies no colour specified by a height/width ratio of 3). When using the height/width option the width of the elipse produced is as specified by the radius parameter, and the height is changed accordingly.

The next and final option availble on the CIRCLE command controls the start and end position of the circle allowing arcs to be drawn. Both start and end values must be between 0 and 1. The way this relates to degrees is shown below:

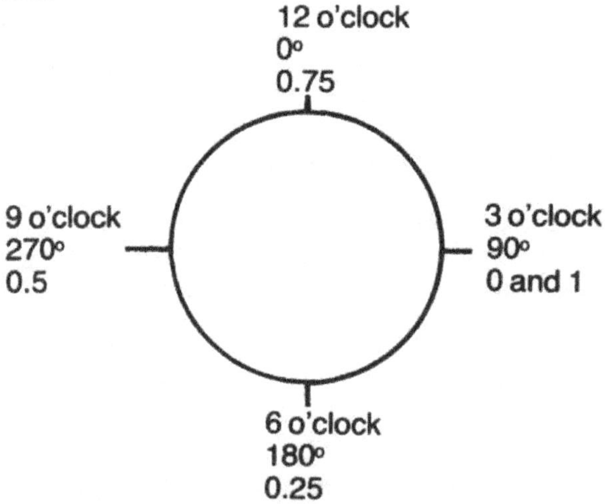

To calculate the parameter (0 — 1) using degrees divide by 360 then, if the result is negative, add 1.

If the end point is smaller than the start point, or either start or end is omitted then a complete circle is drawn starting from the start point and going clockwise. So the final format of circle is:
CIRCLE ([x],[y]), [r], [c], [H/W], [START], [END]

When the start/end options are used the H/W option must also be specified (use 1 for true circles).
Using the CIRCLE command with different radii, H/W ratios and start/end option, almost any curve can be drawn. (See the program on page 110, Circle Example Program.)

DRAW

Another very powerful graphic command available from BASIC is DRAW and it would take a chapter on its own to describe fully.

The DRAW command takes a string (either constant or variable) which contains the commands for DRAW. The commands that can appear in this string are given below:

MOTION

M = Move to an absolute position, x,y.
U = Move up ↑
D = Move down ↓
L = Move left ←
R = Move right →
E = Move 45° ↗
F = Move 135° ↘
G= Move 225° ↙
H =Move 315° ↖

MODE

C = Colour change
A = Angle change
S = Scale change

OPTIONS

N = draw but don't move starting position
B = move starting position but don't draw

OTHER

X = execute substring

The way that the DRAW command works is by having a current starting position that it remembers but you cannot see. Whenever any of the motion commands are encountered in the string this starting position moves either to an absolute position on the screen (same co-ordinates as PSET, x = 0 — 255, y = 0 — 191) or relative to its current position and as it moves, it leaves a trail behind it. Therefore a string, "U10L10D10R10", will draw a closed in box and the start position will be the same as when it started. Before any motion commands have been executed the start position is in the centre of the screen (128, 96). As always there are exceptions to this rule and they are the two options N and B. N causes the line to be drawn as normal but the starting position does not move so that the next command starts from the same position. B causes the starting position to move as normal but it doesn't leave its trail behind.

In reality the B option is not 'move but don't draw' but draw in background color (similar to PRESET) so that if its path takes it over the top of another line, it effectively erases it.

The main difficulty encountered when using the DRAW motion commands is that the commands that move at an angle (E, F, G,H)use a different scale than the others. These lines are approximately 1.42 times longer than those in the horizontal and vertical planes. Therefore, to draw a perfect triangle you use the string "R50U50G50" and you have a perfect triangle but the line that runs at 45° is actually 71 units long.

The mode commands allow the 'current' settings to be altered. When a program is run the current colour is the current foreground colour, the current angle is 0 and the current scale is 4. The colour command (C) can change the current colour to any in the current colour set. The angle mode (A) allows you to rotate what is being drawn 0 — 3 times 45°.
For example, after the command A1 is given then the motion command U will draw a line left while an L command gives a line down, etc.

The scale mode (S) is not as simple as it looks. The number directly following the S (1 — 62) indicates the scaling factor, however each unit of scale represents 0.25 or a quarter, thus 1 = 0.25 : 1 scale, 4 = 1 : 1 scale and 10 = 2.5 : 1 scale, therefore S4 has no effect, S1 — S3 make things smaller and S5 — S62 make things bigger.

The final command available in the DRAW command string is X for eXecute substring. This has an effect similar to GOSUB in that it branches to different commands and then returns to the same spot to continue execution. The command X is followed immediately by the name of the substring to execute. This is a string variable which has been previously assigned a string of DRAW commands. This allows all the basic shapes, e.g. letters, men, etc, to be defined as substrings and these to be executed (drawn) at any time/place in the program. It even allows the size, angle and color of the basic shapes to change from one execution to the next.

Any of the commands may be separated by a semicolon for clarity (eg. U10;L10) but the X command **must** be followed by a semicolon even if it is the last comand in the string.

An example of the DRAW command showing most of its features is given below.

```
10 DO = 2
20 PMODE 1, 1
30 PCLS : SCREEN 1,1
40 B$ = "C4R90C2U10L30D10BL60"
50 DRAW "A0;XB$;A1;XB$;A2;XB$;A3;XB$;"
60 DRAW "S2"
70 DO = DO - 1
80 IF DO > 0 THEN 50 ELSE 80
```

PAINT

The PAINT command does exactly what you think it would do, that is fill in the screen with a specific color. The format of PAINT is:
PAINT ([x],[y]), [c], [b]

Where [x] (0 — 255) and [y] (0 — 191) are the standard graphic co-ordinates and specify where the painting is to start from; [c] is the colour that the area is to be set to and [b] is the colour of the border of the area to be painted. [c] and [b], like all the other colour definitions can be any of the 8 colours but depend on the current colour set. What happens when the PAINT command is executed is that the screen is painted within the confines of the boundary, the colour specified by [c]. If the boundary has the smallest of gaps in it (ie. one element) then the entire screen will be painted.

The boundary can be defined by LINE, DRAW, CIRCLE or by PSETing a shape. The painting starts at the point specified and paints over everything but the border colour.

GET AND PUT

The last two BASIC graphic commands are used together and form a very powerful combination for animated drawings. Basically what they do is get and put sections of the screen into and out of an array. The GET command is the one to use first. This gets the data off the screen and puts it into an array. The format of GET is:
GET ([x1],[y1]) – ([x2],[y2]), [a], G

Where the co-ordinates [x1], [x2], [y1] and [y2] define a rectangle the same as for LINE, [a] is the name of the array in which the data is to be stored and 'G' is an option which specifies full graphic detail (this seems to have no effect, except slightly less space is needed). The size of the array to hold the data must be set by a DIM statement. The array must have two dimensions which between them have enough bytes to contain all the data.
The easiest way to work out the dimensions is make the first dimension equal to [x2] – [x1] and the second dimension [y2] – [y1]. This method is quick to calculate but wastes space. To calculate the most efficient array storage use the one dimension 0 and the other calculate as below.

1. Find the number of elements to be stored
x2 – x1 * y2 – y1
2. If using PMODE 4 or 3 divide this by 8.
If using PMODE 2 or 1 divide this by 16.
If using PMODE 0 divide this by 32.
Round up.
3. Divide this by 5 and round it up again.

The number you have now should be right but may need adjustment by 1, either up or down. Try this number; if you get a FC error when you try the GET command increase the number in the DIM statement by 1, and try again.

Using this saves quite a bit of memory. For example, in PMODE 4, with the G option, if the rectangle being 'got' from the screen was (10, 10) – (30, 30), the first method requires an array DIM (20, 20) or 1210 bytes but the second method requires an array DIM (0, 11) or 11 bytes, less than 10% of the first.

The PUT statement has much the same format as GET.

PUT ([x1],[y1]) – ([x2],[y2]), [a], [action]

Where [x1], [y1], [x2], [y2] and [a] all have the same meaning as for GET. The [action] parameter can have the following values: PSET, PRESET (our old friends), AND, OR or NOT.

With PSET the picture on screen is exactly as it was when the GET statement was used, as would be expected. The PRESET options will erase (PRESET) all the points that are set in the array.

The AND option performs an AND operation on the points set in the array and the points on the screen, then any points set both in the array and on the screen it sets on the screen and all the rest are reset. This option can be used to mask out certain areas of graphics.

The OR option performs an OR operation on the points set on screen and the points set in the array and will set the points that are set in either the screen or the array, resetting all others. this can be used to make two shapes appear on the screen at once.

With the NOT option, it doesn't matter what is in the array even though one must be specified. When the NOT option is used all points on the screen inside the defined rectangle are reversed, ie set points are reset and reset points are set. This can be used to get reverse video effects, etc.

ASSEMBLER/MACHINE CODE GRAPHICS

Using graphics from assembler or machine code is quite a deal harder but startling results can be achieved.

The first thing that must be done is set the mode you want by setting memory location 65472 — 65477 as described at the end of the chapter.

Once one of the 14 modes and the starting address of the screen have been set then there are many different methods to produce graphics.

One way could be to calculate each byte value and save this as data then all your program does is load it into the screen memory. This is a simple program, but it is hard to create the 'picture'. Another way would be to write your own machine code routine to fake the BASIC commands LINE, DRAW, PAINT, etc.

Whichever method you choose, graphics from machine code can be both detailed and fast, much more so than from BASIC.

The following section has details on how each graphic mode stores the pixels and how to use these modes from both BASIC and machine language.

GRAPHICS MODES

This next next section is a description of the 14 graphic modes and how to use them. This page is an explanation of the pages describing the modes. It has the same format and headings but instead of data under the heading it has an explanation of the heading.

MODE number and name of this mode.
ELEMENTS how may elements this mode has. horizontal x vertical
MEMORY MAPPING Where each element is stored

	e.g.	
Addresses from start	+0	"the contents of this address"
i.e. is the start address + 1	+1	

BYTES The number of bytes needed to hold one screen
ADDRESS How to calculate the address for each element. START is the address which the screen starts at, see page 41.

BYTE MAPPING What each bit in each byte of memory relates to
COLORS Which colors are available
SELECT How to set the screen to this mode

NOTE: With byte mapping the elements name in a bit means that if a 1 is there the element is 'ON' and if a zero is there the element is 'OFF', an X means that that bit is not used.

MODES

MODE 1
ALPHANUMERIC — NORMAL TEXT

ELEMENTS 32 x 16
Memory mapping

+0	LINE 1, CHARACTER 1
+1	LINE 1, CHARACTER 2
+32	LINE 2, CHARACTER 1
+33	LINE 2, CHARACTER 2

BYTES = 512
ADDRESS = 32 * Y + X + START

BYTE MAPPING

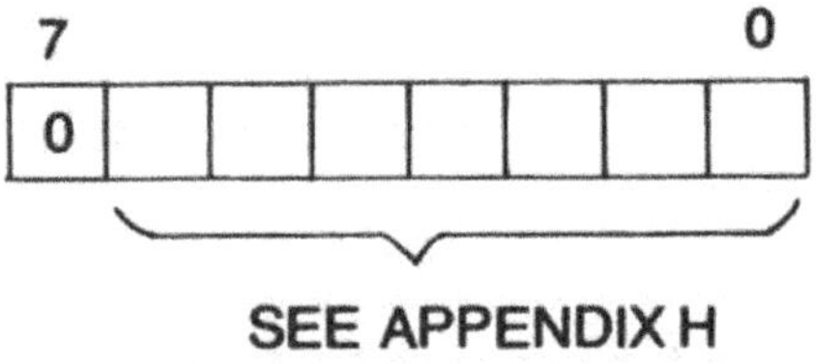

COLOURS:
BORDER = BLACK
FOREGROUND COLOUR SET = 0 — GREEN
COLOUR SET = 1 — ORANGE
SELECT:
This is the standard screen.

MODE 2
SEMI GRAPHIC 4

ELEMENTS 64 x 32
ELEMENT FORMAT

L_3	L_2
L_1	L_0

MEMORY MAPPING

+0	LINE 1, CHARACTER 1
+1	LINE 1, CHARACTER 2
+32	LINE 2, CHARACTER 1
+33	LINE 2, CHARACTER 2

BYTES = 512
ADDRESS = 32 * Y + X + START

BYTE MAPPING

7							0
1	C	C	C	L_3	L_2	L_1	L_0

COLOURS	BORDER	=	BLACK	
	CCC	=	000	GREEN
			001	YELLOW
			010	BLUE
			011	RED
			100	BUFF
			101	CYAN
			110	MAGENTA
			111	RED

SELECT:
SET/RESET when in TEXT mode
Alphanumeric and this mode are together

MODE 3
SEMI GRAPHIC 6

ELEMENTS 64 x 48
ELEMENT FORMAT

L_5	L_4
L_3	L_2
L_1	L_0

MEMORY MAPPING

+0	LINE 1, CHARACTER 1
+1	LINE 1, CHARACTER 2
+32	LINE 2, CHARACTER 1
+33	LINE 2, CHARACTER 2

BYTES = 512
ADDRESS = 32 * Y + X + START

BYTE MAPPING

7							0
C	C	L_5	L_4	L_3	L_2	L_1	L_0

COLOURS BORDER = BLACK

CC =	00	GREEN	COLOUR SET = 0
	01	YELLOW	
	10	BLUE	
	11	RED	
	00	BUFF	COLOUR SET = 1
	01	CYAN	
	10	MAGENTA	
	11	ORANGE	

SELECT:
A = PEEK (65314): POKE 65314, (A and 7) + 16 + X
Where X = 0 for colour set 0
X = 8 for colour set 1
POKE 65476,0: POKE 65474,0 : POKE 65472,0

MODE 4
SEMI GRAPHICS 8

ELEMENTS 64 x 64
ELEMENT FORMAT

A	L_7	L_6
B	L_5	L_4
C	L_3	L_2
D	L_1	L_0

MEMORY MAPPING

+0	ROW A, LINE 1, CHAR 1
+1	ROW A, LINE 1, CHAR 1
+32	ROW B, LINE 1, CHAR 1
+33	ROW B, LINE 1, CHAR 2
+128	ROW A, LINE 2, CHAR 1
+129	ROW A, LINE 2, CHAR 2

BYTES = 2048
ADDRESS = 128 * Y + 32 * ROW + X + START

BYTE MAPPING

	7							0
A	1	C	C	C	L_7	L_6	X	X
B	1	C	C	C	L_5	L_4	X	X
C	1	C	C	C	X	X	L_3	L_2
D	1	C	C	C	X	X	L_1	L_0

COLOURS	BORDER	=	BLACK	
	CCC	=	000	GREEN
			001	YELLOW
			010	BLUE
			011	RED
			100	BUFF
			101	CYAN
			110	MAGENTA
			111	ORANGE

SELECT:
A = PEEK (65314) : POKE 65314, (A AND 7)
POKE 65475,0 : POKE 65475,1 : POKE 65472,0

MODE 5
SEMI GRAPHIC 12

ELEMENTS 64 x 96
ELEMENT FORMAT

A	L_{11}	L_{10}
B	L_9	L_8
C	L_7	L_6
D	L_5	L_4
E	L_3	L_2
F	L_1	L_0

MEMORY MAPPING

+0	ROW A, LINE 1, CHAR 1
+1	ROW A, LINE 1, CHAR 2
+32	ROW B, LINE 1, CHAR 1
+33	ROW B, LINE 1, CHAR 2
+192	ROW A, LINE 2, CHAR 1
+193	ROW A, LINE 2, CHAR 2

BYTES = 3072
ADDRESS = Y * 192 + ROW * 32 + X + START

BYTE MAPPING

	7							0
A	1	C	C	C	L_{11}	L_{10}	X	X
B	1	C	C	C	L_9	L_8	X	X
C	1	C	C	C	L_7	L_6	X	Y
D	1	C	C	C	X	X	L_5	L_4
E	1	C	C	C	X	X	L_3	L_2
F	1	C	C	C	X	X	L_1	L_0

COLOURS	BORDER	=	BLACK	
	CC	=	000	GREEN
			001	YELLOW
			010	BLUE
			011	RED
			100	BUFF
			101	CYAN
			110	MAGENTA
			111	ORANGE

SELECT:
A = PEEK (65314) : POKE 65314, (A AND 7)
POKE 65477, 1 : POKE 65474, 0 : POKE 65472, 0

MODE 6
SEMI GRAPHICS 24

ELEMENTS 64 x 192
ELEMENT FORMAT

A	L_{23}	L_{22}
B	L_{21}	L_{20}
C	L_{19}	L_{18}
D	L_{17}	L_{16}
E	L_{15}	L_{14}
F	L_{13}	L_{12}
G	L_{11}	L_{10}
H	L_9	L_8
I	L_7	L_6
J	L_5	L_4
K	L_3	L_2
L	L_1	L_0

MEMORY MAPPING

+0	ROW A, LINE 1, CHAR 1
+1	ROW A, LINE 1, CHAR 2
+32	ROW B, LINE 1, CHAR 1
+33	ROW B, LINE 1, CHAR 2
+384	ROW A, LINE 2, CHAR 1
+385	ROW A, LINE 2, CHAR 2

BYTES = 6144
ADDRESS = Y * 384 + ROW * 32 + X + STARTS

BYTE MAPPING

	7							0
A	1	C	C	C	L_{23}	L_{22}	X	X
F	1	C	C	C	L_{13}	L_{12}	X	X
G	1	C	C	C	X	X	L_{11}	L_{10}
L	1	C	C	C	X	X	L_1	L_0

COLOURS	BORDER	=	BLACK	
	CCC	=	000	GREEN
			001	YELLOW
			010	BLUE
			011	RED
			100	BUFF
			101	CYAN
			110	MAGENTA
			111	ORANGE

SELECT:
A = PEEK (65314) : POKE 65314, (A AND 7)
POKE 65477, 1 : POKE 65475, 1 : POKE 65472, 0

MODE 7
GRAPHICS 64 x 64 FOUR COLOUR

MEMORY MAPPING

+0	ROW 1, COLUMN 1—4
+1	ROW 1, COLUMN 5—8
+16	ROW 2, COLUMN 1—4
+17	ROW 2, COLUMN 5—8
+1022	ROW 64, COLUMN 57—60
+1023	ROW 64, COLUMN 61—64

BYTES = 1024
ADDRESS = ROW * 16 + FIX ((COLUMN-1)/4) +START

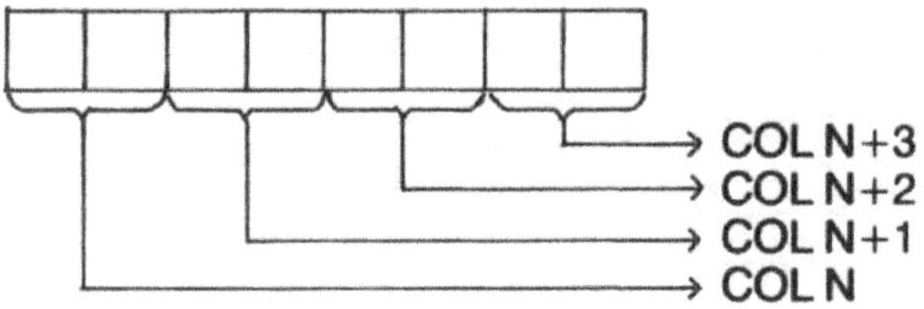

COLOURS	BORDER	=	GREEN	COLOR SET = 0	
			BUFF	COLOUR SET = 1	
	CC	=	00	GREEN	COLOUR SET = 0
			01	YELLOW	
			10	BLUE	
			11	RED	
			00	BUFF	COLOUR SET = 1
			01	CYAN	
			10	MAGENTA	
			11	ORANGE	

SELECT:
A = PEEK (65314) : POKE 65314, (A AND 7) + 128 + C
Where C = 0 for COLOUR SET 0
C = 8 for COLOUR SET 1
POKE 65473, 1 : POKE 65474, 0 : POKE 65476, 0

MODE 8

GRAPHICS 128 x 64 TWO COLOUR

MEMORY MAPPING

+0	ROW 1, COLUMN 1-8
+1	ROW 1, COLUMN 9-16
+15	ROW 1, COLUMN 120-128
+16	ROW 2, COLUMN 1-8
+1022	ROW 64, COLUMN 112-119
+1023	ROW 64, COLUMN 120-128

BYTES = 1024

ADDRESS = ROW*16 + FIX((COLUMN − 1)/8) + START

BYTE MAPPING

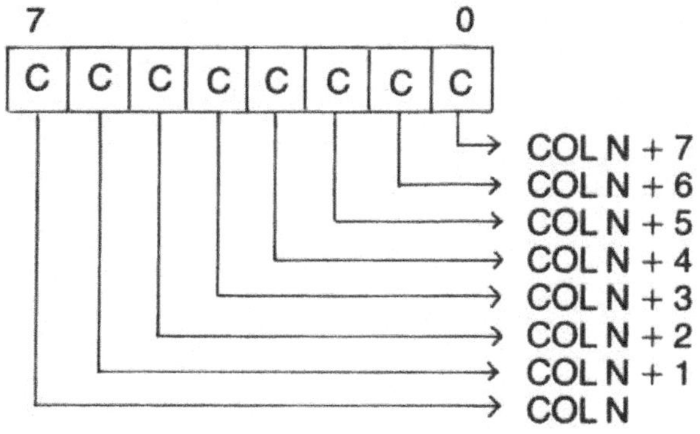

COLOURS			
BORDER =		GREEN	COLOUR SET = 0
		BUFF	COLOUR SET = 1
	C = 0	BLACK	COLOUR SET = 0
	1	GREEN	
	0	BLACK	COLOUR SET = 1
	1	BUFF	

SELECT:

A = PEEK (65314) : POKE 65314, (A AND 7) + 128 + 16 + C

Where C = 0 for COLOUR SET = 0

C = 8 for COLOUR SET = 1

MODE 9
GRAPHICS 128 x 64 FOUR COLOUR

MEMORY MAPPING

+0	ROW 1, COL 1-4
+1	ROW 1, COL 5-8
+31	ROW 1, COL 61 - 64
+32	ROW 2, COL 1-4
+2046	ROW 64, COL 57-60
+2047	ROW 64, COL 61-64

BYTES = 2048
ADDRESS = ROW * 32 + FIX ((COLUMN-1)/4)
+ START

BYTE MAPPING

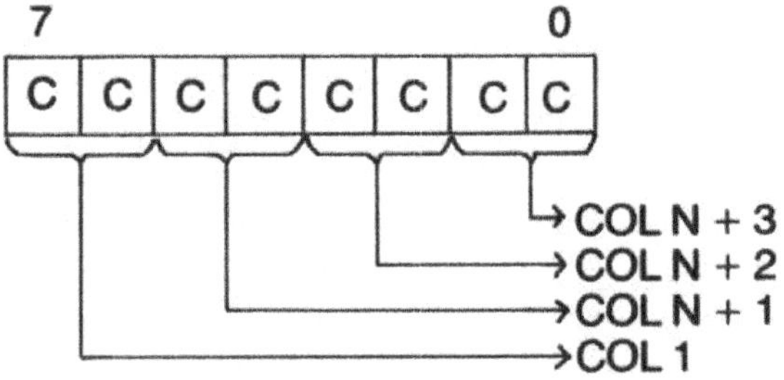

COLOURS	BORDER	=	GREEN	COLOUR SET = 0
			BUFF	COLOUR SET = 1
		CC = 00	GREEN	COLOUR SET = 0
		01	YELLOW	
		10	BLUE	
		11	RED	
		00	BUFF	COLOUR SET = 1
		01	CYAN	
		10	MAGENTA	
		11	ORANGE	

SELECT:
A = PEEK (65314) : POKE 65314, (A AND 7) + 128 + 32 + C
Where C = 0 for COLOUR SET = 0
C = 8 for COLOUR SET = 1
POKE 65472, 0 : POKE 65475, 0 : POKE 65476, 1

MODE 10

GRAPHICS 128 x 96 TWO COLOUR

MEMORY MAPPING

+0	ROW 1, COLUMN 1-8
+1	ROW 1, COLUMN 9-16
+15	ROW 1, COLUMN 120-128
+16	ROW 2, COLUMN 1-8
+1534	ROW 96, COLUMN 113-120
+1535	ROW 96, COLUMN 121-128

BYTES = 1536

ADDRESS = ROW * 16 + FIX ((COLUMN-1)/8) + START

BYTE MAPPING

7							0
C	C	C	C	C	C	C	C

COLOURS			
BORDER	=	GREEN	COLOUR SET = 0
		BUFF	COLOUR SET = 1
	C = 0	BLACK	COLOUR SET = 0
	1	GREEN	
	0	BLACK	COLOUR SET = 1
	1	BUFF	

SELECT:

PMODE0

or

A = PEEK (65314) : POKE 65314, (A AND 7) + 128 + 32 + 16 + C

POKE 65476, 0 : POKE 65475, 1 : POKE 65473, 1

MODE 11
128 x 96 FOUR COLOUR

MEMORY MAPPING

EACH BYTE HOLDS 4 COLUMNS
BYTES = 3072
ADDRESS = ROW * 32 + FIX ((COLUMN-1)/4) + START

BYTE MAPPING

7			0
CC	CC	CC	CC

COLOURS			
BORDER =		GREEN	COLOUR SET = 0
		BUFF	COLOUR SET = 1
	CC = 00	GREEN	COLOUR SET = 0
	01	YELLOW	COLOUR SET = 0
	10	BLUE	COLOUR SET = 0
	11	RED	COLOUR SET = 0
	00	BUFF	COLOUR SET = 1
	01	CYAN	COLOUR SET = 1
	10	MAGENTA	COLOUR SET = 1
	11	ORANGE	COLOUR SET = 1

SELECT:
PMODE 1
or
A = PEEK (65314) : POKE 65314, (A AND 7) + 128 + 64 + C
POKE 65477, 1 : POKE 65474, 0 : POKE 65472, 0

MODE 12
GRAPHICS 128 x 192 TWO COLOUR

MEMORY MAPPING
EACH BYTE HOLDS 8 COLUMNS
BYTES = 3072
ADDRESS = ROW * 16 + FIX ((COLUMN-1)/8) + START

BYTE MAPPING

7							0
C	C	C	C	C	C	C	C

COLOURS	BORDER	=	GREEN	COLOUR SET = 0
			BUFF	COLOUR SET = 1
	C = 0		BLACK	COLOUR SET = 0
	1		GREEN	COLOUR SET = 0
	0		BLACK	COLOUR SET = 1
	1		BUFF	COLOUR SET = 1

SELECT:
PMODE 2
or
A = PEEK (65314) : POKE 65314, (A AND 7) + 128 + 64 + 16 + C
POKE 65477, 1 : POKE 65474, 0 : POKE 65473, 1

MODE 13
GRAPHICS 128 x 192 FOUR COLOUR

MEMORY MAPPING
EACH BYTE HOLDS 4 COLUMNS
BYTES = 6144
ADDRESS = ROW * 32 + FIX ((COLUMN-1)/4) + START

BYTE MAPPING 7 (left) … 0 (right)

CC	CC	CC	CC

COLOURS	BORDER =		
		GREEN	COLOUR SET = 0
		BUFF	COLOUR SET = 1
	CC = 00	GREEN	COLOUR SET = 0
	01	YELLOW	
	10	BLUE	
	11	RED	
	00	BUFF	COLOUR SET = 1
	01	CYAN	
	10	MAGENTA	
	11	ORANGE	

SELECT:
PMODE 3
or
A = PEEK (65314) : POKE 65314, (A AND 7) + 128 + 64 + 32 + C
POKE 65477, 1 : POKE 65475, 1 : POKE 65472, 0

MODE 14

GRAPHICS 256 x 192 TWO COLOUR

MEMORY MAPPING

EACH BYTE HOLDS 8 COLUMNS

BYTES 6144

ADDRESS = ROW * 32 + FIX ((COLUMN-1)/8) + START

BYTE MAPPING

7							0
C	C	C	C	C	C	C	C

COLOURS	BORDER =		GREEN	COLOUR SET = 0
			BUFF	COLOUR SET = 1
		C = 0	BLACK	COLOUR SET = 0
		1	GREEN	
		0	BLACK	COLOUR SET = 1
		1	BUFF	

SELECT:

PMODE 4

or

```
A = PEEK (65314) : POKE 65314, (A AND 7) + 128 + 64 + 32 + 16 + C
POKE 65477, 1 : POKE 65475, 1 : POKE 65472, 0
```

CHAPTER 3

SOUND

There are a variety of methods to make your DRAGON roar. There are the two BASIC commands, SOUND and PLAY as well as generating sound using a machine code routine.

The BASIC command SOUND is useful for creating sound effects in your programs. You may want to prompt people that they are required to enter data, maybe even different tones for different types of data and another when a mistake is made.

Try this line for when people make mistakes:

```
FOR I = 150 TO 10STEP -10 : SOUND I, 1 : NEXT
```

Sound is fine for special effects but what about some music. The PLAY command is very powerful and designed for just that. The string of commands needed for PLAY is very easy to produce from a sheet of music. Notes, sharps and flats, length of notes and pauses are directly converted, even the tempo and the volume can be changed.

Notes can be defined in different ways; by their letter (A — G) (with sharps and flats) or by number. Using numbers is a more concise way of defining notes but makes the string harder to read for those who are musically minded. The relationship between number and letter is shown in figure 4.1 and how both of these are related to a keyboard in figure 4.2

NUMBER	NOTE
1	C
2	C#/D−
3	D
4	D#/E−
5	E/F−
6	F/E#

NUMBER	NOTE
7	F#/G−
8	G
9	G#/A−
10	A
11	A#/B−
12	B

Figure 4.1 Musical Number/Note Table

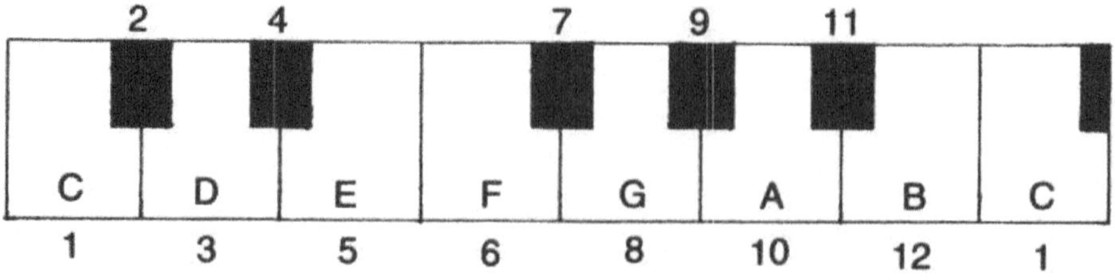

Fig 4.2 Keyboard

Note that C# is the same note as D– and D# the same as E– etc., but be warned DRAGON does not recognise C– as being B or B# as being C.

The play command has a five octave range. When notes are played they are played from the current octave (the initial current octave is 2). Octaves are changed using the O option and once the octave has been set it remains at that until either it is reset by another O option or the machine is switched off. The same is true for volume, length and tempo.

The length of notes is selected by the L option. The value following L is the reciprocal of the length of the note. Therefore, L2 means a half note or 2 notes per beat and L4 means a quarternote or 4 notes per beat, etc. As in sheet music a note followed by a dot means that that note is to be half as long again. For example, L2. specifies notes of three-quarters duration (half + quarter).

The P option lets you pause between notes and the number which follows the P has the same effect as in L options, the only difference being you can't add a dot at the end. To make a pause of half as long again use two P's in a row. e.g. P2P4.

The T option lets you change the overall speed of music or how many beats there are in every second. The number following T multiplied by 0.4 gives you how many beats there are per second or 2.5 times the number of beats per second you want gives you the value to use in the T option.

The PLAY command, like DRAW, has the ability to execute substrings. This is done with the X option followed by the name of the string to be executed. Note that a semicolon (;) must be placed after the dollar sign in the string name (it is optional between all other commands). After the substring has been executed control returns to the option after the semicolon.

Instead of using a number after some commands (T, V, L, O) one of the following symbols may be used:
+ — increase the current value by one.
– — decrease the current value by one.
> — multiply the current value by two.
< — divide the current value by two.

Note that the program will halt with an error if the value of these options goes outside their legal range (ie., T = 1 — 255, V = 0 — 31, L = 1 — 255, O = 1 — 5).
Here are a couple of songs, already programmed, to give you some idea.

```
10 '** GOD SAVE THE QUEEN **
20 A$="T3;L3DDEL3.C#L6DL3E"
30 B$="F#F#GL3.F#L6EL3DEDC#DP2"
40 C$="L3AAAL3.AL6GL3F#GGGL3.GL6F#L3E"
50 D$="L3F#L6GF#EDL3.F#L6GL3A"
60 E$="L6BGL2F#ED"
70 PLAY A$+B$+C$+D$+E$
```

```
10 '** ENGLISH COUNTRY GARDEN **'
20 A$="O4T4;L4CL6CO3L8BL4AAGL6GL8FL4E"
30 B$="L8EFL4GCDFL2EL8DL2C"
40 C$="O4L6CL8DL6CO3L8AL6BL8AL4G"
50 D$="O4L4CL6CO3L8BL4AO4DO3L2BL8AL2G"
60 E$="O3L6EL8FL4GO4L6CO3L8BL4AAL6GL8AL6GL8FL4E"
70 PLAY "XA$;XB$;XA$;XB$;"
80 PLAY "XC$;XC$;XD$;XE$;XB$;"
```

Using Machine Language

Producing your own sounds from machine code programs is a little harder to do. The only control you have over the sound is to switch the speaker on and off. To produce audible sounds the speaker must be turned on and off at certain rates (frequencies) approximately 20Hz – 18KHz, rembering the limitations of your speaker and ears.

The speaker is connected to the PIA and is controlled through the PIA registers. These registers are located in memory from &HFFOO to &HFF3F.

For sound we are only interested in &HFF22 and &HFF23. Bit 3 of the &HFF23 register is the sound enable/disable register. To enable the one-bit sound this bit must be set to 0. Bit-1 of the register &HFF22 is the bit that actually controls the speaker. However, it must first be set to be an output bit, not an input bit. The short assembly program below sets up the PIA registers ready for production of sound.

```
7002    B6  FF23    LDA     $FF23
7005    84  F3      ANDA    #$F3
7006    B7  FF23    STA     $FF23
700A    F6  FF22    LDB     $FF22
700D    CA  02      ORB     #$02
700F    F7  FF22    STB     $FF22
7012    8A  04      ORA     #$04
7014    B7  FF23    STA     $FF23
```

After the PIA registers have been set up as above, then toggling bit 2 of register &HFF22 turns the speaker on and off. (Be careful that no other bits are affected by toggling as they cotrol the VDG.) The easiest way to accomplish this is shown below.

```
7055    B6  FF22    LDA     $FF22
7058    88  02      EORA    #$02
705A    B7  FF22    STA     $FF22
```

As you will no doubt have noted the addresses look like they come from a bigger program. This program is in the HANDY ROUTINES CHAPTER (called SOUND) and is quite good for all types of effects.

When using sounds in a BASIC games program it is best to keep the sounds short as the processor is tied up producing the sound and the program has to wait until it has finished.

When using sounds in machine language programs you can do some processing in between the toggling of the speaker and so 'longer' notes can be played without disturbing the flow of the game.

Reproducing Human Speech

Here is a program which allows you to store sounds in digital form. Sounds are analysed and stored away to be replayed at a later date. Any sound including music, noise and voices can be stored this way.

The heart of the program is a small machine language routine which does the sampling, storing and replaying of the sounds. This is included in assembler format as well as in a BASIC program as DATA statements.

The sounds are entered through your cassette player and replayed through your TV set so no special equipment is needed.

Since the cassette port can have only one of two values (a high level (1) and a low level (0)) the speech is stored as a series of values between 0 and 255 (this range is used because it is the range of values that can be stored in a single byte of the computer's memory). Each value is simply the length of time between changes of the level of the cassette port, ie. suppose the cassette port is low (0) then we start counting until it goes high (1) at this stage we save the count in memory and reset the counter to zero. We then start counting again until the port goes low again save the count, reset it to zero, etc. This process is continued until the available memory is filled up.

The stored speech takes up 6K of memory and will last about 1 to 4 seconds depending upon the content.

HOW TO RUN THE BASIC PROGRAM

When the program is run there will be a short pause while the machine code is put into memory. It is placed at the top of the available memory (at locations 28672 onwards) and protected with a CLEAR statement. When this is done a menu of options will be displayed and pressing one of the keys I, O, R, A, S, L will select the option you desire.

I — INPUT SPEECH

The speech is input from the cassette port using one of two methods described below.

When the I key is pressed the computer will display the message "PRESS ANY KEY TO START", at this point the cassette should be readied to send the speech to the computer. When all is ready press any key and the computer will start to store the speech. The computer will display a graphic screen which will fill up with what looks like rubbish but is actually the values that make up the input speech. When the screen is full the computer will return you to the menu.

Actually getting the speech to the computer is very simple and can be done in one of two ways, both using your cassette recorder.

Method 1:

Prepare a cassette with the speech you want the computer to record using either the built in microphone or an external microphone (note the better the sound of this recording the better the results will be when the computer plays back the speech, so it is usually best to use an external microphone).

Once the cassette is ready it is simply played into the computer just like a program cassette. Note that since the program will not start the cassette motor you should unplug the remote jack from the cassette recorder.

Method 2:

This is similar to the above except that you don't need to record what you want to say you just say it directly to the computer. Firstly your cassette recorder must be able to send what it is recording to the external speaker jack. If it can do this then all you need to do is put the machine into record mode and talk into the microphone when the computer is inputting speech.

To put the cassette recorder into record mode without a cassette in it you must open the cassette door and look inside. You should see a small switch at the back left hand side. If this is pressed in then with the RECORD and PLAY buttons pressed in the cassette will be in record mode.

O — OUTPUT SPEECH

This will call the machine language subroutine to send the recorded speech to the speaker in the television set. The graphic screen containing the speech is displayed while it is talking and if you look carefully you will see a small white line moving around the screen. This line is tracing the speech on the screen as it is sent to the speaker.

R — REPEATED SPEECH OUTPUT

This is similar to O except that it will repeat the same speech over and over until a key is pressed.

A — ANALYSE SPEECH

Since the sound is stored as a sequence of numbers we can draw a graph of them and see the distribution of frequencies in what was said to the computer. The graph is drawn on the highest resolution graphics screen with the vertical scale being the total count that each number occurs (ie. the higher the line the more times that number occured), while the horizontal scale is the numbers (from 0 to 255, see above for how these numbers are calculated).

When this graph is finished the screen will change colour and the computer will wait until you hit a key. You will probably notice on this graph that the left side of the screen is full of tall lines while the right side of the screen is fairly empty. This is because in a given time interval you can fit more short counts (hence small numbers) than long ones. To try and correct this problem a new graph is drawn, after you press a key, in which the vertical scale is the total time used by each interval length. When this graph is finished the computer will again wait for a key to be pressed at which time it will return to the menu.

S — SAVE SPEECH (to cassette)

This gives you the option to save the speech in the digital form the computer uses to store it.

The computer will ask you for a name to use when it saves your speech to cassette. After you press ENTER it will save the speech in digital form on the cassette so make sure your recorder is ready and that the microphone and remote plugs are back in.

L — LOAD SPEECH (from cassette)

This will load a previously saved block of data representing speech from the cassette. The computer will prompt you for a name (optional). Note this can only be used to load blocks previously saved with the S command.

TIPS

To get the best results you will need to experiment with the volume levels on your cassette recorder. Since it may take a number of tries to find the optimum setting we suggest that you make a recording of some speech first and use method 1 to input the speech initially. Remember the better the sound on the cassette the better the results will be.

On some cassette recorders the silences between words will have enough background noise in them so that the computer will record the noise. Since the computer is only using two levels when the speech is outut this background noise will be reproduced at the same volume level as the speech. This can be overcome somewhat by adjusting the volume level but if you have a noisy cassette recorder you will have to live with it. If your recorder does produce silent gaps between words you will notice that no matter how long the gap between two words, when the speech is played back the gap will have been cut to a much shorter value. This is caused by having only values between 1 and 255 for the lengths between changes.

MAKING OTHER PROGRAMS TALK

To use the machine code routines in your own program it would be easiest to save the machine code together with the speech that you want to use on tape.

RUN the above program then press BREAK when at the command menu.

Prepare your cassette recorder for saving a program and type in:
CSAVEM "SCODE",&H7000,&H705D,&H7029
This will save the machine code to tape.

RUN the program again. Input the speech you wish to use and save it to tape — note that you can save as many blocks as you like and include them all in your program.

Now suppose you have saved the machine code and two blocks of speech to tape, and you wish to have a program that puts these two blocks at memory location &H4000 and &H5800 respectively then in your program you will need the following:

```
10 CLEAR 200, &H4000 : 'PROTECT MEMORY
20 CLOADM "SCODE" : 'LOAD MACHINE CODE
30 CLOADM "name1", &H4000–&H0600
```

This line loads the first block of speech (with name name1) at location &H4000 onward (the normal location is &H0600 so the offset to put it at &H4000 is &H4000–&H0600).

```
40 CLOADM "name2", &H5800–&H0600
```

Similarly for the second block.

When you want to output the first block of speech you should use

```
POKE &H7000,&H40 : POKE &H7001,0
EXEC &H7029
```

To output the second block you need the lines

```
POKE &H7000,&H58 : POKE &H7001,0
EXEC &H7029
```

THE TALKING DRAGON

```
10 ' SPEECH PROGRAM
20 ' FOR THE DRAGON
30 PCLEAR 8:CLEAR 200,&H7000
40 CLS:PRINT" STORING MACHINE CODE"
50 DIM A(255)
60 SS=&H0600:SE=SS+&H17FF
      ' START & END OF SPEECH MEM
70 READ IS,OS,I:IS=IS+I:OS=OS+I
80 READ P
90 IF P>=0 THEN POKE I,P:I=I+1:GOTO 80
100 '
110 ' COMMAND LOOP
120 SOUND 40,1:AUDIO OFF:CLS:SCREEN 1,0
130 PRINT"COMMAND KEYS:"
140 PRINT" I-INPUT SPEECH"
150 PRINT" O-OUTPUT SPEECH ONCE"
160 PRINT" R-OUTPUT SPEECH REPEATEDLY"
170 PRINT" A-ANALYSE SPEECH"
180 PRINT" S-SAVE SPEECH"
190 PRINT" L-LOAD SPEECH"
200 GOSUB 730
210 ON INSTR("IORSLA",A$)
      GOTO 260,340,390,440,490,540
220 PRINT" INVALID COMMAND"
230 GOTO 200
240 '
250 ' SPEECH INPUT
260 PRINT"PRESS ANY KEY TO START"
270 PMODE 4,1:PCLS
280 AUDIO ON:GOSUB 730
290 SCREEN 1,1
```

```
300 EXEC IS' INPUT SPEECH
310 GOTO 120
320 '
330 ' OUTPUT SPEECH ONCE
340 PMODE 4,1:SCREEN 1,1
350 AUDIO ON:EXEC OS' OUTPUT SPEECH
360 GOTO 120
370 '
380 ' OUTPUT SPEECH REPEATEDLY
390 PMODE 4,1:SCREEN 1,1:AUDIO ON
400 EXEC OS:IF INKEY$="" THEN 400
410 GOTO 120
420 '
430 ' SAVE SPEECH TO CASSETTE
440 INPUT"NAME";A$
450 CSAVEM A$,SS,SE,0
460 GOTO 120
470 '
480 ' LOAD SPEECH FROM CASSETTE
490 INPUT"NAME";A$
500 CLOADM A$
510 GOTO 120
520 '
530 ' ANALYSE SPEECH
540 PMODE4,5:PCLS:SCREEN 1,1
550 FOR I=0 TO 255:A(I)=0:NEXT I
560 FOR I=SS TO SE
570 P=PEEK(I)
580 IF A(P)<192 THEN PSET(P,192-A(P))
590 A(P)=A(P)+1
600 NEXT I
610 SCREEN 1,0:GOSUB 730
620 FOR I=1 TO 255
630 A(I)=A(I)*I'CORRECT VALUES
640 IF A(I)>P THEN P=A(I)
650 NEXT I
660 P=191/P
670 FOR I=1 TO 255
680 LINE(I,191)-(I,191-P*A(I)),PSET
690 NEXT I
700 GOSUB 730
710 GOTO 120
720 '
730 ' SUBROUTINE TO WAIT FOR KEY PRESS
740 A$=INKEY$:IF A$="" THEN 740
750 IF ASC(A$)=3 THEN STOP
760 RETURN
770 '
780 ' SPEECH ROUTINE OFFSETS FROM START OF CODE
790 DATA 4,41
800 ' CODE START ADDRESS
810 DATA &H7000
820 ' SPEECH MEMORY START HIGH&LOW BYTES
830 DATA 6,0
840 ' SPEECH MEMORY LENGTH HIGH&LOW BYTES
850 DATA 24,0
860 ' SPEECH SUBROUTINES
870 DATA 26,80,206,255,32,174,140,244,16,174,140,242
```

```
880 DATA 95,92,141,72,100,196,37,249,231,128,95,
        92,141,62,100,196
890 DATA 36,249,231,128,49,62,38,232,57,26,80,
        206,255,32,204,52
900 DATA 63,167,93,76,167,95,231,67,174,140,197,
        16,174,140,195,230
910 DATA 128,99,132,134,128,167,196,141,19,90,38,
        247,99,132,230,128
920 DATA 111,196,141,8,90,38,249,49,62,38,228,57,57
930 DATA -1
```

THE TALKING DRAGON MACHINE LANGUAGE ROUTINE

```
0001 0E00                        NAM SPEECH
                         * SPEECH INPUT AND OUTPUT ROUTINES
                         * SUBROUTINE INPUT MONITORS THE
                         * CASSETTE INPUT LINE AND RECORDS
                         * THE LENGTHS OF THE HIGHS AND LOWS
                         *
                         * SUBROUTINE OUTPUT TAKES THESE
                         * LENGTHS AND OUTPUTS HIGHS AND
                         * LOWS TO THE TV SET
                         *
                         * THE SPEECH MEMORY LOCATION AND
                         * SIZE ARE SPECIFIED AT TSTART
                         * AND LENGTH RESPECTIVELY
                         *
                         * EACH LOOP IS 23 CYCLES LONG
                         *
0002 FF20                PIA     EQU $FF20          PIA LOCATION
                         * BIT 0 IS THE CASSETTE INPUT LEVEL
                         * BITS 7-1 CONTROL THE D/A CONVERTER

0003 0E00                        ORG $7000          START PROGRAM AT 7000 HEX
0004 7000 0600           TSTART  FDB $0600          START OF TEXT
0005 7002 1800           LENGTH  FDB $1800          LENGTH OF SPEECH
                         * INPUT SPEECH SUBROUTINE
0006 7004                INPUT
0007 7004 1A50                   ORCC #$50          DISABLE INTERRUPTS
0008 7006 CEFF20                 LDU #PIA           POINTER TO PIA
0009 7009 AE8CF4                 LDX TSTART,PCR     POINTER TO START OF MEMORY
0010 700C 10AE8CF2               LDY LENGTH,PCR     MEMORY LEFT FOR SPEECH
0011 7010                ILOOP
                         * TIME HIGH SIGNAL
0012 7010 5F                     CLRB               RESET TIME COUNTER
0013 7011                IH
0014 7011 5C                     INCB               INCREMENT TIME COUNTER
0015 7012 8D48                   BSR DELAY          DELAY
0016 7014 64C4                   LSR ,U             TEST BIT0 OF PIA
0017 7016 25F9                   BCS IH             LOOP IF STILL SET

0018 7018 E780                   STB ,X+            SAVE TIME COUNT
                         * TIME LOW SIGNAL
0019 701A 5F                     CLRB               RESET TIME COUNTER
0020 701B                IL
0021 701B 5C                     INCB               INCREMENT TIME COUNTER
0022 701C 8D3E                   BSR DELAY          DELAY
0023 701E 64C4                   LSR ,U             TEST BIT0 OF PIA
0024 7020 24F9                   BCC IL             LOOP IF STILL CLEAR

0025 7022 E780                   STB ,X+            SAVE TIME COUNT
0026 7024 313E                   LEAY -2,Y          2 BYTES OF MEMORY USED
0027 7026 26E8                   BNE ILOOP          LOOP IF NOT OUT OF MEMORY
```

```
7028 39                 RTS

                  * OUTPUT SPEECH

7029           OUTPUT
7029 1A50               ORCC #$50        DISABLE INTERRUPTS
702B CEFF20             LDU #PIA         POINTER TO PIA
702E CC343F             LDD #$343F
7031 A75D               STA -3,U         SELECT DAC
7033 4C                 INCA              BEING CAREFULL ABOUT
7034 A75F               STA -1,U         MODIFYING INTERRUPTS
7036 E743               STB 3,U          SOUND ENABLE
7038 AE8CC5             LDX TSTART,PCR   POINTER TO START OF MEMORY
703B 10AE8CC3           LDY LENGTH,PCR   MEMORY FREE FOR SPEECH
703F           OLOOP
               * OUPUT HIGH SIGNAL
703F E680               LDB ,X+          GET TIME COUNT
7041 6384               COM ,X           FLASH NEXT BYTE(TO SEE IT)
7043           OH
7043 8680               LDA #$80         OUTPUT LEVEL
7045 A7C4               STA ,U           SEND TO PIA
7047 8D13               BSR DELAY        DELAY
7049 5A                 DECB              DECREMENT TIME COUNTER
704A 26F7               BNE OH           LOOP UNTIL 0

704C 6384               COM ,X           RESTORE NEXT BYTE
               * OUTPUT LOW SIGNAL
704E E680               LDB ,X+          GET TIME COUNT
7050           OL
7050 6FC4               CLR ,U           SET OUTPUT LEVEL TO 0
7052 8D08               BSR DELAY        DELAY
7054 5A                 DECB              DECREMENT TIME COUNTER
7055 26F9               BNE OL           LOOP UNTIL 0

7057 313E               LEAY -2,Y        2 BYTES OF MEMORY USED
7059 26E4               BNE OLOOP        LOOP IF MEMORY LEFT
705B 39                 RTS               RETURN TO BASIC

705C 39        DELAY    RTS               DELAY 12 CLOCK CYCLES

705D                    END
```

CHAPTER 4

WHAT IS MACHINE CODE?

At the heart of every micro computer, is a central microprocessor. It's a special chip called the CPU (Central Processing Unit). This is the 'brain' of the computer. Each type of CPU has its own language and instructions. These instructions go together to make up machine language. In other words machine language is the only language which the CPU can understand. It is the native tongue of the machine.

All the instructions are numbers of one or two bytes long. So how does the DRAGON understand BASIC programming language?

To answer this question, you must first see what happens inside the DRAGON. Apart from the CPU there are also two types of memory; RAM and ROM. RAM (Random Access Memory) is the memory where the programs you enter are stored.RAM is volatile, which means that unless there is a power supply to the memory it 'forgets' everything. The other type of memory is ROM (Read Only Memory). This type of memory has the operating system in it. The operating system is a huge machine language program stored in ROM (so that it can't be changed and is automatically run when the DRAGON is turned on).

The operating system is in charge of 'organizing' all RAM in your machine for various tasks. It can be thought of as the 'intelligence and personality' of the DRAGON as it does all the 'talking' to you.

All the commands that are available in BASIC are simply reorganized by another big machine language program called the interpreter, which is also stored in ROM.

The interpreter simply deciphers each BASIC statement one by one and executes the appropriate machine language program, unless you do something wrong in which case it puts an error message on the screen. So why bother with machine language if somebody else has already written these vast programs to make your computer 'friendly' and 'talk' a language which is easy for you to learn?

Well, programs written in machine language are very fast, use less memory and are usually more complex. You may have noticed with the programs you have bought, those that were written in machine language have more graphical detail and run so much faster than those written in BASIC.

If at this stage you are still interested in machine language programming but don't really understand what I am talking about then probably the best way to go about learning machine language is to read the other book in this series DRAGON MACHINE LANGUAGE FOR THE ABSOLUTE BEGINNER.

THE CPU

The CPU used in the DRAGON is the M6809, one of the most powerful 8-bit micros available today. The power of the M6809 over other 8-bit CPUs is by specific improvements in architecture, software and hardware over its predecessor, the M6800.

On the architectural side, the M6809 has a multitude of registers. Each register will be discussed in detail later but basically they are:
— two 8-bit accumulators, A and B, which can be used together to form one 16-bit accumulator, D
— two 16-bit index-registers, X and Y
— two 16-bit stack pointers, S and U
— one 8-bit Direct Page register, DP
— one 16-bit Program Counter, PC
— one 8-bit Condition Code register, CC
The software features are probably the main reason for the M6809's power. The very complex addressing modes almost need a full chapter by themselves to describe and I will introduce them to you briefly later on. Specific instructions which are not common on 8-bit CPUs include:
— an 8x8 unsigned multiply which generates a 16-bit number.
— a 2-byte instruction to push or pull any or all of the registers onto or from either stack (S or U).
— a 16-bit add, subtract, load, store and compare which uses the D accumulator.
— instructons to add any of the accumulators (A, B, D) to any of the index registers or stack pointers (X, Y, S, U).
— instructions for exchanges or transfers between any two like size CPU registers.

The hardware improvements over the M6800 include:
— either internal clock (M6809) or external clock (M6809E).
— FIRQ, Fast Interrupt ReQuest which doesn't save all the registers.
— BS, Bus Status and BA, Bus Available, used together to provide interrupt acknowledge and bus status.
— Q and E, the clock lines. Q leads E by a quarter cycle (90°). These two together provide 4 effective timing edges.
— MRDY, Memory ReaDY, for interfacing with slow memories.
— DMA REQ, Direct Memory Access REQuest, input control line to suspend processor execution and free buses for direct memory access such as a peripheral device, etc.

To show the relative power of the M6809 the table below shows time comparisons for eight different software operations on the popular CPUs used today.

OPERATION / CPU	I/O HANDLER	CHARACTER SEARCH	COMPUTED GOTO	DOUBLE SHIFT RIGHT 5 BITS	16 BIT ADDS	8 BIT ADDS	16x16 MULT	MOVE BLOCK (64 BYTES)
6809 2.0MHz	28	287.5	34.5	15	325	180	82	344.5
Z80 4.0 MHz	38.3	220.5	73.3	41	518	323	267	342
9900 3.0 MHz	72	661	98	22	537	537	42	537
6800 2.0 MHz	24.5	404	64.5	19	993.5	498.5	409.5	1123.5
8080 3.0 MHz	52.7	506.7	96.7	91.3	732	492	784	841
8085 2.0 MHz	79	760	145		1098	738	1176	1262

REGISTERS

The internal register structure of the M6809 is shown below followed by a brief description of what each register is used for.

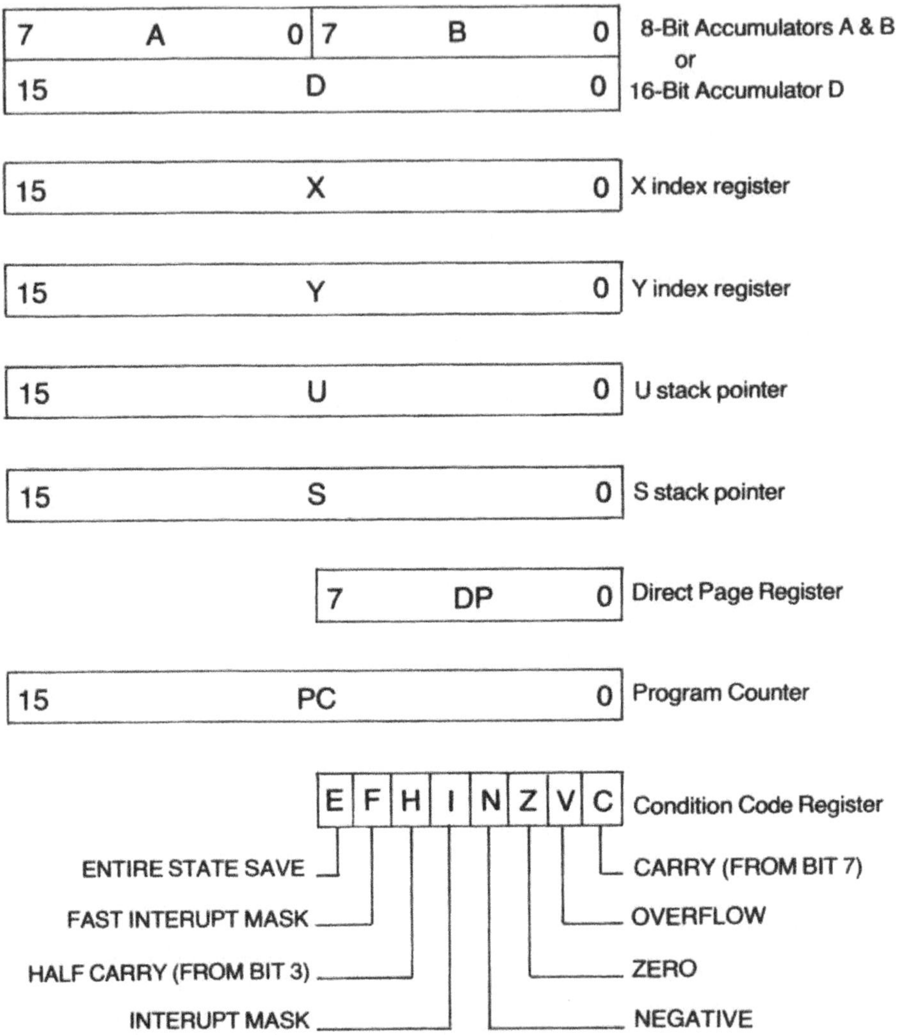

ACCUMULATORS

There are two 8-bit accumulators which are used to hold the current data to work with. These two can be combined to form one 16-bit accumulator, the D accumulator. Almost every instruction uses one of these registers and most data manipulation instructions (ADD, SUB, etc.) work only on the accumulators.

INDEX REGISTERS

These two 16-bit registers are used mainly to 'point' to sections of data and can be accessed automatically during load and store instructions (see Indexed Addressing Mode) with all sorts of fancy tricks to make large data manipulation very fast. They can also be used to store 16-bit numbers temporarily while the accumulators are manipulating other data.

STACK POINTERS

The M6809 is one of the few 8-bit CPUs to have two stackpointers. With most CPUs, if the user wanted to implement a stack he would have to do some very tricky manoeuvering because the stack pointer is needed for interrupts and other system usage. With the two stack pointers, one can be used solely for the system leaving the other for the user's use.

DIRECT PAGE REGISTER

This register has very few instructions that can access it directly, namely EXG and TFR but it is accessed automatically every time direct addressing mode is used (see appropriate section).

PROGRAM COUNTER

The program counter controls the execution of a program and contains the address of the next instruction to be executed. This register cannot be accessed directly but is automatically changed during branching operations, etc. The program counter can be used with an offset in indexed addressing mode allowing position independent code.

CONDITION CODE REGISTER

This register contains the 'status' of the last operation. Most instructions will modify some bit of this register and conditional branches use these bits for their decision on whether to branch or not.

ADDRESSING MODES

You are about to see what makes the M6809 such a powerfull CPU. The addressing modes of the M6809 is one of the main factors in the M6809's power. The M6809 has 59 different instructions which utilize 10 fundamental addressing modes bringing the total number of unique instructions to 1464. An addressing mode describes how the data, that the instruction is going to use, is to be found.

INHERENT

This is sometimes called implied addressing and is the simplest mode as the instructions which use this mode do not need any data. Instructions such as INC, DEC and ASL work on the accumulators only and do not need any data.

IMMEDIATE

Immediate addressing is where the data to be used with the instruction immediately follows the instruction. The analogy in BASIC would be a constant, whereas the other modes that follow are analogous to various types of variables.

EXTENDED

This mode of address requires two bytes, following the instruction, which contain the address of the data to be used. With extended addressing a full 64K of memory can be accessed.

DIRECT ADDRESSING

This is a limited form of extended addressing and only requires one byte to follow the instruction. This is sometimes called zero page addressing as only the first 255 bytes of memory can be accessed but reduces the time and space that a program needs to run in as only the low byte needs to be specified. The advantage of the M6809 over most other CPUs is that it allows this 'zero page' to be moved about in memory by setting the Direct Page register which in effect becomes the high byte of the address.

OP CODE (1 or 2 bytes)
DATA OPERAND (1 or 2 bytes)

(A) IMMEDIATE ADDRESSING

OP CODE (1 or 2 bytes)
HI ADDRESS BYTE
LOW ADDRESS BYTE

(B) EXTENDED ADDRESSING

OP CODE (1 or 2 bytes)
LOW ADDRESS BYTE

(C) DIRECT ADDRESSING
NOTE: HI ADDRESS IS IN DP REG.

RELATIVE ADDRESSING

There are two main types of relative addressing: Branch Relative and Program Counter Relative and using the two allows completely relocatable code to be written.

BRANCH RELATIVE

There are two types of branch instructions, short and long, both of which use a two's complement (signed) relative address offset. Upon execution of the branch the offset is added to the program counter's contents to form the address of the next instruction to be executed. Note that when the instruction is executing the program counter is already pointing to the next sequential instruction. The short branch uses one byte offset which allows a branch length of −128 through to +127, whereas the long branch uses a two byte offset allowing branches of −32768 through to +32767 in length.

PROGRAM COUNTER RELATIVE

This is really an indexing mode but is covered briefly here as it, in combination with branch relative addressing, is needed to write relocatable code. Basically, what is done is to use the index addressing mode which allows you to have a 16-bit register and an 8- or 16-bit offset field and specify the PC as the register to use (see constant offset indexed addressing).

INDEXED ADDRESSING

There are four basic forms of index addressing, each of which can use the four pointer registers (X, Y, S, U). They are: zero-offset, constant offset (which can also use PC), accumulator offset and auto-increment/decrement.

OP CODE (1 or 2 bytes)
POST BYTE
OFFSET (0, 1 or 2 bytes)

GENERAL INDEXED ADDRESSING INSTRUCTION FORMAT

As you can see the instruction is always followed by the post byte which specifies the form of indexing to use and register to use as the pointer that will be used in determining the effective operand address. The post byte may or may not be followed by an offset.

ZERO-OFFSET INDEXING

This type of indexing uses the pointer registers as the effective operand address, with no offset. The post byte specifies the zero-offset mode and which register to use.

CONSTANT OFFSET INDEXING

This type of indexing is similar to other machines' indexing modes as any of the pointer registers (X, Y, S, U, PC) can be used and the signed offset can be 5, 8 or 16 bits. The post byte contains the pointer register and offset size. When a 5-byte offset is used this is included as part of the post byte and therefore is the most efficient as it uses less bytes and CPU cycles compared to other constant offset modes.

ACCUMULATOR-OFFSET INDEXING

This form of indexing is similar to the constant offset form except that the contents of one of the accumulators (A, B, D) is added to the specified index register (X, Y, S, U). The obvious advantage of this is that the offset can be calculated just prior to the indexing operation.

AUTO-INCREMENT/DECREMENT INDEXING

This mode of indexing is a blessing as it eliminates the need to increment/decrement the index register with a separate instruction when stepping through memory or moving blocks of memory. When incrementing, the register is changed after the contents have been used to find the effective address and when decrementing,the register is changed before the contents are used. So it is post-increment and pre-decrement. The post byte specifies the auto-imcrementing/ decrementing, the pointer register to use and the amount to increment/ decrement by (1 for 8-bit data or 2 for 16-bit data).

POST-BYTE REGISTER BIT								INDEXED ADDRESSING MODE
7	6	5	4	3	2	1	0	
0	R	R	O F F S E T					EA=R±4 bit offset
1	R	R	0	0	0	0	0	R+
1	R	R	*	0	0	0	1	R++
1	R	R	0	0	0	1	0	−R
1	R	R	*	0	0	1	1	−−R
1	R	R	*	0	1	0	0	EA=R±0 offset
1	R	R	*	0	1	0	1	EA=R±ACCB offset
1	R	R	*	0	1	1	0	EA=R±ACCA offset
1	R	R	*	1	0	0	0	EA=R±7 bit offset
1	R	R	*	1	0	0	1	EA=R±15 bit offset
1	R	R	*	1	0	1	1	EA=R±D offset
1	X	X	*	1	1	0	0	EA=PC±7 bit offset
1	X	X	*	1	1	0	1	EA=PC±15 bit offset

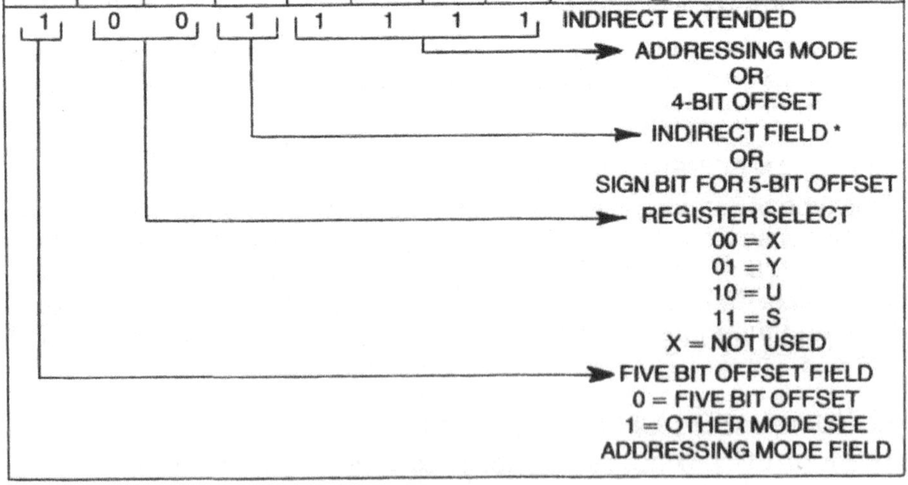

* INDIRECT FIELD (see next section)

INDIRECT ADDRESSING

With indirect addressing the operand's address (where the data is stored) is contained at the location specified by the operation. Indirect addressing can be used with any of the indexing modes except for auto-increment/decrement by 1 (see table above) as well as with extended addressing. To specify indirect addressing in the indexing modes, set bit 4 of the post byte. To get indirect addressing using extended mode the post byte must have:

bit 7 = 1 — not 5-bit offset mode
bit 6, 5 = 0 — no register used
bit 4 = 1 — indirect field
bit 3-0 = 1 — extended mode

When using indirect extended mode the opcode (for indexing mode) is followed by the post byte (&H9F) followed by the address which contains the address of the operand.

REGISTER ADDRESSING

The last addressing mode covered is register addressing which is used on the EXT and TFR instructions. With these instructions the post byte contains two fields: bits 0 — 3 specify the destination register and bits 4 — 7 specify the source register.

EXG or TFR OPCODE
POST BYTE

(A) INSTRUCTION FORMAT

7	6	5	4	3	2	1	0
SOURCE REGISTER				DESTINATION REGISTER			

(B) POST BYTE FORMAT

(C) FIELD DESIGNATIONS

4 BIT FIELD	REGISTER
0000	ACC D
0001	X
0010	Y
0011	U
0100	S
0101	PC
1000	ACC A
1001	ACC B
1010	CC
1011	DP

USING MACHINE LANGUAGE PROGRAMS ON THE DRAGON

ENTERING AND RUNNING MACHINE LANGUAGE PROGRAMS.

There are only two ways to enter information directly into memory: POKEing and CLOADMing. These two commands allow you to actually set memory locations to certain values.

If you are not going to be writing a multitude of machine language programs the easiest way to store, enter and run your programs, while they are being developed, is to have them as DATA in a BASIC program. This makes editing them quite simple especially if you use a convention such as only have one instuction/operand per DATA statement. When your program is finished, immediately after doing a RUN in BASIC, CSAVEM your program for future use. Remember, whenever you are mixing BASIC programs with machine code programs, to set the upper limit that BASIC can use with the CLEAR statement, otherwise the programs can destroy each other.

On the other hand if you are going to be doing a lot of machine language programming then you need a monitor program, or better still a full Assembler/Editor. If you look around you will find a few assembler/editors on the market but if you want to get out of it cheaply, I have included a simple monitor program with which you can enter, modify, and display parts of memory as well as find a string of characters in memory, execute a machine language program and convert numbers from hexadecimal to decimal and vice-versa.
The commands, their format and a description of each is given below followed by the program listing and a brief outline of how the program works.

M — M[address] — Memory examine and change.
— when this command is used, the address, the contents of the address and a hyphen are displayed. The two arrow keys on the left, display the next higher or lower address respectively. If at any time you want to change the contents of a memory address hit C and enter the value (in hex.). To return to command level, key ENTER directly after a hyphen.

D — D[address] — Display memory.
— This will display the memory in groups of four bytes followed on the same line by the four characters which represent by the memory's contents. After one screen full of memory is displayed, the listing waits for you to enter — a space will give you another screen full of information
— any other key will return to the command mode.

F — F[b address] [e address] [string] — Find a string in memory.
— This searches memory beginning at [b address] through to [e address] for the character string, [string]. All the addresses which point to the start of the string, if there are multiple strings, are displayed. If [string] is not found, nothing is printed.

C — C D [number]
— C H [number]
— This converts the number [number] to either hex or decimal depending on whether H (decimal to hex) or D (hex to decimal) is specified.

J — J[address] — Jump to Machine Language Program.
— This causes the machine language program starting at [address] to be executed.

E — E — Exit to BASIC.
NOTE: All addresses must be four hex digits.
Formats must be exactly as shown, ie. no spaces between the command letter and the first address (except for C) and 1 space between all other parameters.

LISTING

```
10 '** MACHINE CODE MONITOR **
20 PRINT "COMMANDS: M, D, F, C, J, E";
30 INPUT CL$:CT$=LEFT$(CL$,1)
40 IF CT$="" THEN 20
50 CT=INSTR("MDFCJE",CT$)
60 IF CT=0 THEN 20
70 ON CT GOSUB 100,300,400,500,600,700
80 GOTO20
100 BA=VAL("&H"+MID$(CL$,2,4))
110 IF BA<0 OR BA>&HFFFF THEN 900
120 AC=PEEK(BA)
130 PRINT HEX$(BA)" "HEX$(AC)" -";
140 MC$=INKEY$:IFMC$=""THEN 140
150 MC=ASC(MC$)
160 IF MC=94 THEN BA=BA+1:PRINT:GOTO110
170 IF MC=10 THEN BA=BA-1:PRINT:GOTO110
180 IF MC=13 THEN PRINT:RETURN
190 IF MC$<>"C" THEN 140
200 INPUT MC$
210 NB=VAL("&H"+MC$):IFNB<0 OR NB>&HFF THEN PRINT:RETURN
220 POKE BA,NB
```

```
230 BA=BA+1:GOTO120
300 BA=VAL("&H"+MID$(CL$,2,4)
310 IF B<0 OR BA>&HFFFF THEN 900
320 CNT=0
325 PRINT HEX$(BA);
330 FORI=0 TO 3:PRINT" "HEX$(PEEK(BA+I));:NEXTI:
    PRINT"  ";
340 FORI=0 TO 3:PRINT" "CHR$(PEEK(BA+I));:NEXTI:PRINT
345 BA=BA+4
350 IF CNT<12 THEN CNT=CNT+1:GOTO325
360 PRINT:CNT=0
370 MC$=INKEY$:IF MC$=""THEN370
380 IF MC$=" "THEN 325 ELSE RETURN
400 BA=VAL("&H"+MID$(CL$,2,4))
410 EA=VAL("&H"+MID$(CL$,7,4))
420 IF BA<0 OR BA>&HFFFF OR EA<BA OR EA>&HFFFF THEN 900
430 FS$=MID$(CL$,12):FL=LEN(FS$)
440 FORI=BA TO EA
450 IF PEEK(I)<>ASC(LEFT$(FS$,1)) THEN 490
460 FORJ=I TO I+FL-1:IF PEEK(J)<>ASC(MID$(FS$,J-I+1,1))
    THEN 490
470 NEXTJ
480 PRINT HEX$(I)
490 NEXTI:RETURN
500 IF MID$(CL$,3,1)<>"D" THEN 520
510 PRINT VAL("&H"+MID$(CL$,5)):RETURN
520 IF MID$(CL$,3,1)<>"H" THEN RETURN
530 PRINT HEX$(VAL(MID$(CL$,5))):RETURN
600 BA=VAL("&H"+MID$(CL$,2))
610 IF BA<0 OR BA>&HFFFF THEN 900
620 EXEC BA
630 RETURN
700 END
900 PRINT "ILLEGAL HEX ADDRESS"
910 RETURN
```

VARIABLES

AC	— Address Contents
BA	— Begin Address
CL$	— Command Line
CT, CT$	— Command Type
EA	— End Address
FL	— Find string Length
FS$	— Find String (string searched for)
MC, MC$	— Modify Command
NB	— New Byte

10 INITIALIZE
20–80 MAIN CONTROL LOOP
100–230 MEMORY EXAMINE AND MODIFY
300–380 DISPLAY MEMORY
400–490 FIND A STRING
500–530 CONVERT NUMBERS
600–630 JUMP TO MACHINE LANGUAGE PROGRAM
700 END
900–910 ERROR IN ADDRESS

This is only a sample of what a machine language monitor can do. Other functions which are very useful (but outside the scope of this book) are an assembler, disassembler, block moves, etc.

HANDY ROM ROUTINES

These following routines are included in your DRAGON's ROM and can easily be used in your machine language programs.
Each routine has a name which is used to identify it followed by an entry address in hexadecimal. However, an EXEC or a USR function call will not invoke all of these routines correctly. Some need entry conditions such as having the A accumulator and the X index register initialized.

A brief summary of what the routine does and what the entry and exit conditions are, is also included. At the end of the section there is a list of the variables (memory locations) that are used in the routines and a brief word on what they do.

INIT &HBB40

Initialize hardware interfaces such as printer, cassette, video, memory, etc.

Shouldn't be used except for auto-start cartridge programs.

SETUP &HBB88

Sets up BASIC system variables such as keyboard debounce, cassette leader length, printer variables, etc.

BLINK &HBBB5

Decrements location 008F and when this counter reaches zero the cursor is toggled from black to green or vice-versa.

TOUCH &H8E12

Write the character in the accumulator A onto the cassette.

BYTE-IN &HBDAD

Gets 8 bits off the cassette and puts them into the A accumulator.

BIT-IN &HBDA5

Gets the next bit on tape and puts it into the carry bit.

BLKIN &HB93E

Reads a block from cassette
CONDITIONS
ENTRY — cassette must be on and in bit synchronization (see CSRDON)
— CBUFAD(7E) contains the buffer address.

EXIT — BLKTYP(7C) contains the block type
— BLKLEN(7D) contains number of data blocks in the block (0 — 255).
— Z = 1, ACC = 0 if no errors CSRERR(81) = 0
— Z = 0, ACC = 1 if checksum error CSRERR(81) = 1
— Z = 0, ACC = 2 if memory error CSRERR(81) = 2
— Unless there was an error X points to the last byte in the buffer
— U, Y preserved, all others changed.
Interrupts are masked.

BLKOUT &HB999

Writes a block to cassette
CONDITIONS
ENTRY — Tape should be up to speed
— a leader of &H55's should have been written if this is the first block to be written after motor on
— CBUFAD(7E) — buffer address
— BLKTYP(7C) — contains block type
— BLKLEN(7D) — contains number of bytes in block
EXIT — X points to last byte in buffer
— All registers modified
Interrupts are masked.

WRTLDR &HBE6A

Turns cassette on and writes a leader.
CONDITIONS
ENTRY — none
EXIT — U preserved, all others modified.

CSRDON &H8021

Turns cassette on and gets in bit sync.
CONDITIONS
ENTRY — none

EXIT — FIRQ and IRQ are masked.
— U, Y preserved, all others modified.

CHROUT &HB54A

Outputs a character
CONDITIONS
ENTRY — DEVNUM(6F) set to −2 (printer) or 0 (screen).
— A character to be used.
EXIT – All registers except CC preserved.

JOYIN &HBD52

Sample joystick ports
CONDITIONS
ENTRY — none
EXIT — Y preserved, all others changed.
— POTVAL (15A) through to POTVAL + 3 (15D) contain the position of joysticks.

POLCAT &HBBE5

Polls keyboard for a character
CONDITIONS
ENTRY — none
EXIT
— Z = 1, A = 0 — no key pressed.
— Z = 0, A = key code — if key seen.
— B and X preserved, all others modified.

VARIABLES FOR ABOVE ROUTINES

BLKLEN(7D) length of cassette block
BLKTYP(7C) type of cassette block
0 = File Header
1 = Data
FF = End of File
CBUFAD(7E) cassette buffer address
CSRERR(81) cassette error type
0 = no errors
1 = checksum error
2 = memory error
DEVNUM(6F) device for CHROUT
−2 = printer
0 = screen
POTVAL(15A) 4 bytes holds current joystick position
15A = left joystick up/down
15B = left joystick left/right
15C = right joystick up/down
15D = right joystick left/right

HANDY MEMORY LOCATIONS IN THE DRAGON

START ADDRESS DEC	HEX	DESCRIPTION	END ADDRESS DEC	HEX
00025	0019	Address of start of BASIC program	00026	001A
00027	001B	Address of Start of variable storage also address −1 is end of Basic program	00028	001C
00029	001D	Address of start of array storage	00030	001E
00031	001F	Address of start of free memory	00032	0020
00033	0021	Address of start of string stack	00034	0022
00035	0023	Address of BASIC upper limit	00036	0024
00039	0027	Highest available RAM address	00040	0028
00108	006C	Current column position of cursor		
00111	006F	Device number DEVNUM		
00113	0071	Warm start flag RSTFLAG &H0 = Condition before cartridge program Starts created by BASIC &H12 = Do warm start &H55 = If RSTVEC points to a NOP then execute from address RSTVEC else start BASIC		
00114	0072	Warm start Vector RSTVEC	00115	0073
00116	0074	Highest physical memory address	00117	0075
00124	0076	Block type BLKTYP 0 = file header 1 = data FF = end of file		
00125	007D	Bytes in block BLKLEN		
00126	007E	Buffer address CBUFAD also program end +1 after CLOADM	00127	007F
00128	0080	Check sum		
00129	0081	CSRERR		
00140	008C	Sound frequency		
00141	008D	Sound duration	00142	00BE
00157	009D	Transfer address after CLOADM	00158	009E
00182	00B6	Current Pmode		
00256	0100	SWI 3 vector	00258	0102
00259	0103	SWI 2 vector	00261	0105
00262	0106	SWI 1 vector	00264	0108
00265	0109	NMI vector	00267	010B
00268	010C	IRQ vector	00270	010E
00271	010F	FIRQ vector	00273	0111
00289	0121	Pointer to BASIC command Token Table	00290	0122
00290	0123	Pointer to BASIC command Jump Table	00292	0124
00294	0126	Pointer to BASIC function Token Table	00295	0127
00296	0128	Pointer to BASIC function Jump Table	00297	0129
00337	0151	KEYBOARD Recover Table	00345	0159

00337	0151	Bit cleared if any bit in same column cleared							
		7	6	5	4	3	2	1	0
00338	0152		ENTER	X	P	H	@	8	0
00339	0153		CLEAR	Y	Q	I	A	9	1
00340	0154			Z	R	J	B	:	2
00341	0155			↑	S	K	C	;	3
00342	0156			↓	T	L	D	,	4
00343	0157			←	U	M	E	—	5
00344	0158			→	V	N	F	•	6
00345	0159			space	W	O	G	/	7

00346	015A	Joystick 0 — left x position		
00347	015B	Joystick 1 — left y position		
00348	015C	Joystick 2 — right x position		
00349	015D	Joystick 3 — right y position		
00466	01D2	CASSETTE file name	00473	01D9
00474	01DA	CASSETTE buffer	00731	02D8
00485	01E5	Transfer address used in CSAVEM	00486	01E6
00733	02DD	Keyboard buffer	00988	03DC
01024	0400	Text screen memory	01535	05FF
01536	0600	GRAPHICS Screen memory (in 8 pages of 1536 bytes each)	13823	35FF
03072	0C00	User RAM note can start anywhere between 03072 (0C00) and 13224 (3600) depending on graphics pages.	32767	7FFF
32816	8033	BASIC command word table	33064	8128
33108	8154	BASIC command jump table	33225	81C9
33226	81CA	BASIC function word table	33359	824F
33360	8250	BASIC function jump table	33427	8293
33449	82A9	BASIC error message table	33499	82DB
33504	82E0	BASIC interpretor	49151	BFFF
49152	C000	cartridge slot	65279	FEFF
65280	FF00	PIA (Parrallel I/O Adapter)	65521	FFF1
65522	FFF2	SWI 3 vector (contains 0100)	65523	FFF3
65524	FFF4	SWI 2 vector (contains 0103)	65525	FFF5
65526	FFF6	FIRQ vector (contains 010F)	65527	FFF7
65528	FFF8	IRQ vector (contains 010C)	65529	FFF9
65530	FFFA	SWI 1 vector (contains 0106)	65531	FFFB
65532	FFFC	NMI vector (contains 0109)	65533	FFFD
65534	FFFE	RESET vector (contains B3B4)	65535	FFFF

HOW BASIC STORES VARIABLES

At the top of user RAM a space is reserved for the string stack. This space can be increased or decreased by the CLEAR command. Possible reasons for changing the size of the stack are:

Increase — you have a short program which uses a lot of strings and string manipulations.

Decrease — you have a large program (ie. running out of memory for the program itself) that does not use many strings.
Immediately below this space is the variable stack.
For every new variable used the variable stack grows downwards 6 bytes and contains — for:
Strings : byte 1 — length of string
bytes 2, 5, 6 — reserved for system
bytes 3, 4 — address, in string stack, of the first byte of the string
Numerics : byte 1 — exponent
bytes 2-5 — mantissa
byte 6 — reserved for system

STRING STACK

Whenever a string variable is made, even if it is for the same variable name, it is put on 'top' of the stack. So when a string variable is assigned a different string, the new string is put on 'top' of the stack and the address in the variable stack is updated. Note that the old string is still in the string stack but cannot be accessed. This means that a program that does a lot of string manipulations, wastes a lot of space on the string stack.

```
10 A$ = "HELLO"
20 B$ = "DRAGON"
30 A$ = A$ + B$
```

	7	7	7	7	7	7	7									7					
	F	F	F	F	F	F	F									F					
	F	F	F	F	F	F	F									E					
Stack Adr.	F	E	D	C	B	A	9	8	7	6	5	4	3	2	1	0	F	E	D	C	B	A
After line 10	H	E	L	L	O																	
After line 20	H	E	L	L	O	D	R	A	G	O	N											
After line 30	H	E	L	L	O	D	R	A	G	O	N	H	E	L	L	O	D	R	A	G	O	N

EXAMPLE OF HOW THE STRING STACK 'GROWS'
After line 10, A$'s pointer will be 7FFF
After line 20, A$'s pointer will be 7FFF and B$'s pointer will be 7FFA.
After line 30, A$'s pointer will be 7FF4 and B$'s pointer will be 7FFA.

HOW NUMERICS ARE STORED IN THE VARIABLE STACK

Numbers are stored in 5 bytes, 1 byte exponent and 4 bytes mantissa. The most significant bit of the most significant byte of the manitissa is assumed to be 1 (as floating point mantissas are always normalized), and this bit is used to store the sign of the mantissa (positive = 0, negative = 1).

To convert a decimal number (X) into the internal representation follow the simple procedure below.
1. If X = 0 then all bits are set to 0.
2. Convert decimal to binary — leave decimal point in its place.
3. Exponent (1 byte)
If there are any digits to the left of the binary point then the exponent equals the number of digits to the left.
If the first digit on the right is a one then the exponent is zero otherwise the exponent equals the complement of the number of zeros, going left to right, up to the first digit.
Add hex 80 to the exponent calculated so far.
4. Now remove the binary point and all leading zeros and add zeros to the end until there are 32 digits in all.
5. If the original number was positive, change the first 1 to a 0.
6. Group into 8 groups of 4 and convert to hex.

HOW TO ACCESS BASIC VARIABLES FROM MACHINE LANGUAGE PROGRAMS

The first thing that has to be done if you are going to mix machine language and BASIC is to reserve a space at the top of memory by using the CLEAR command. Failure to reserve space may lead to BASIC programs 'destroying' your machine language programs or vice-versa.

After reserving space for your program it must then be put into memory. This can be done by CLOADM, POKEs or a BASIC program.

There are two ways to start it; EXEC and USR. The main difference between the two commands is that with USR you can pass parameters from BASIC to machine language and have values returned from machine language to BASIC.

Using EXEC simply causes a jump to a memory address. When the machine language program executes an RTS, control will be returned to BASIC at the next command if inside a program, or at command level if the EXEC was entered directly.
On the other hand, USR is used as a normal BASIC function, ie A = USR1(B). The advantage of using a USR call to start up the machine language program is that it allows data to be transferred. After a USR call the A register contains the type of data that was used in the call (A = 0 — numeric data, A = non-zero — string data) and the X register points to the actual data.
For numeric data the X register points to the FAC (Floating point ACcumulator) which contains the number in the format described above.

It is possible to convert this to an integer by calling the ROM routine INTCNV (hex 8B30) which returns a 16-bit two's compliment integer in the D register. If the data was a string, INTCNV causes an overflow error and control is returned to BASIC.

For string data the X register points to the 5-byte descriptor as described above.

The USR function always returns at least one value to BASIC. If the machine language program does not explicitly return a value, the value is the same one as that passed to the program. In general, the type of data returned is the same as that passed, in the same location and in the same format.

However, regardless of the original data, an integer may be returned by loading the D register with a 16-bit two's compliment integer and calling the ROM routine GIVABF (hex 8C37).

There are a few rules when modifying string variables and returning them to BASIC.
The length of the string may be changed by changing the length byte in the string's descriptor. Strings may be shortened by this but a USR routine should never lengthen a string. To allow variable length strings to be returned, the string should be forced to a maximum length of 255 before the USR call. For example:
A$ = USR0 (STRING$ (" ", 255))
The starting address may be modified by changing the address in the descriptor. However, the new address should generally be that of a memory location contained in the original string and the length reduced by the appropriate amount. It is possible to swap the addresses of two strings which would be useful for a fast string sorting routine.
The GOLDEN RULE when modifying strings is to never let two strings intercept.

Apart from using the USR call it is possible to transfer data to and from machine language programs by POKEing data into memory locations reserved by the CLEAR command. The address to POKE into is also known by the machine language routine and can be used and modified in any way and then left to be PEEKed at by the BASIC program after the machine language routine has finished.

CHAPTER 5

PERIPHERALS

JOYSTICKS

The two ports marked for joysticks are really four analogue to digital converters. One left/right right converter, one up/down right converter, one left/right left converter, and one up/down left converter. These ports are accessed in BASIC by the command JOYSTK with the parameter 0 — 3 selecting which AD converter to sample. Memory location 65280 indicates if the fire buttons have been pushed. The values of the location are: 255 means no buttons pushed, 254 means the right button, 253 the left and 252 means both fire buttons have been pushed.
Apart from plugging joysticks into these ports, other analogue devices may be used and the information converted to digital form.

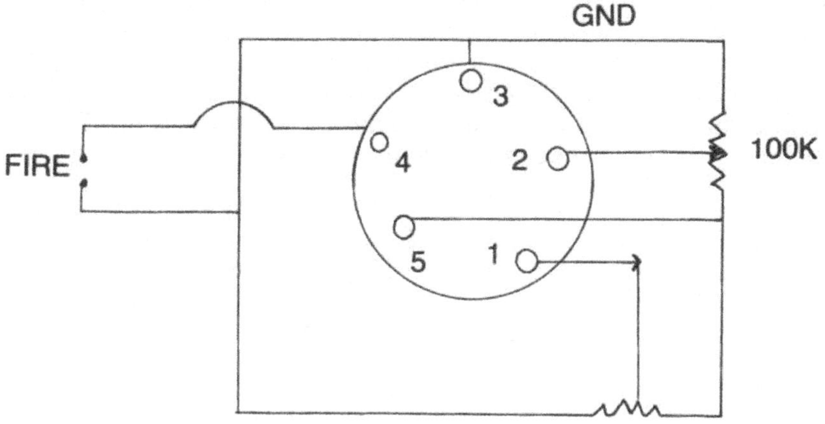

Figure 6.1

Figure 6.1 gives details for the pin connections when joysticks are used and using this diagram and some initiative virtually any analogue device could be connected. Useful devices to interface could be a thermister for a digital thermometer, multi-turn potentiometers for a trackball or with strings and pullies for a pen tracer. The possibilities are endless, the only limitations being your imagination and initiative.

PRINTER

The parallel printer port can be used from BASIC by the LLIST command and also the PRINT#−2 command. The port can be used not only for printer connections but also other devices that accept parallel data such as a down loader etc. Pin connections for the printer port are shown in Figure 6.2.

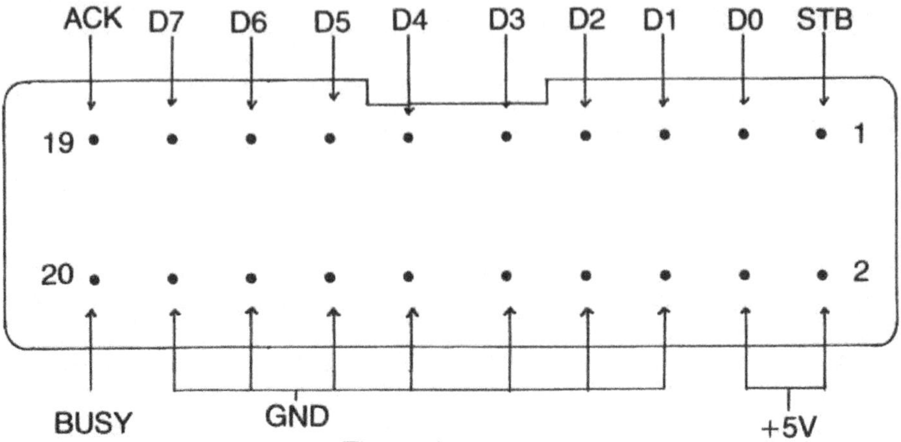

Figure 6.2

CASSETTE

The cassette port is used from BASIC by the commands relating to saving and loading programs and the INPUT#−1 and PRINT#−1 commands. Having the ability to switch the motor on and off could be used with another relay to control home electrical appliances. This could be a heater and using a thermister wired into a joystick port your DRAGON could be used as a thermostat for energy saving. The pin connections for the cassette ports are shown in Figure 6.3

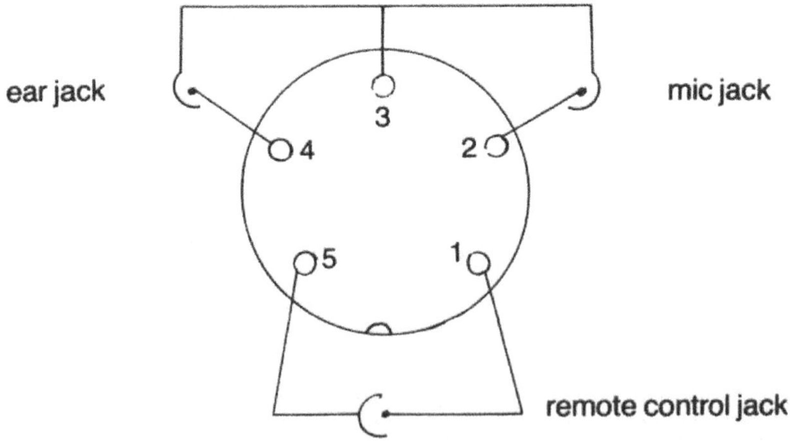

FIGURE 6.3

MONITOR/TV

There are two ways to get video signals on a screen. There are connections for a standard UHF TV or an RGB monitor. When an RGB monitor is being used the sound can be heard from the cassette interface, via the lead normally connected to the microphone socket. If a TV is being used it should be tuned to approximately channel 44UHF.

EDGE CONNECTOR

The edge connector is designed for using ROMpack games, disk drives, memory expanders, etc but could also be used for any hardware that you can think of to interface. Building circuitry with address decoders etc. would allow you to have memory mapped I/O, program and use your own EPROMs etc.

The connections of the board edge are shown in Figure 6.4

Figure 6.4

PIN			
1	−12V	10 — 17	D0 — D7
2	+12V	18	R/W
3	HALT	19 — 31	A0 — A12
4	NMI	32	C000 — FEFF (chip select)
5	RESET	33, 34	0V
6	E(6809 CLOCK)	35	Analogue in
7	Q(6809 CLOCK)	36	FF40 — FF5F select
8	CB1	37 — 39	A13 — A15
9	+5V	40	Turn off internal ROM

CHAPTER 8

HANDY ROUTINES AND TIPS

SPEEDING THINGS UP

There are three different speeds at which the DRAGON can run: 0.9MHz, 0.9/1.8MHz and 1.8MHz. The standard speed at which the DRAGON runs is 0.9MHz. The faster speed of 0.9/1.8MHz is achieved by having the CPU operate at 0.9MHz when accessing RAM and 1.8MHz when accessing ROM. This means when running BASIC programs where most of the processing is done in ROM, and RAM is only used for data and programs, etc. the program will run quite a bit faster. However, machine language programs which operate almost entirely in RAM do not achieve an equivalent step up in speed. The 0.9/1.8 speed can be activated by POKEing 65495 with 0 and can be returned to normal by POKEing 65495 with 126.

The 1.8MHz speed will effectively double the speed of both BASIC and machine language programs alike. The problem with this speed is that the VDG (Video Display Generator) gets out of synchronization with the CPU and the display turns to rubbish. This simple machine language routine will get the CPU and VDG back into synchronization.

```
B7   FFD8     STA     $FFD8    Exit 1.8 MHz mode
13            SYNC             Synchronize CPU & UDG
39            RTS              Return
```

This should be entered, saved on cassette and tested before trying to enter the 1.8MHz mode. Even though the display is meaningless while the DRAGON is in the 1.8MHz mode, anything put on the screen can be viewed once 0.9 MHz mode is returned. The 1.8MHz can be entered by POKEing 65497 with zero and exited as described above.
The characteristics of the three modes are:

	MODE		
	0.9 MHz	0.9/1.8 MHz	1.8 MHz
SPEED	1.0	≈ 1.35	2.0
display	yes	yes	no*
cassette	yes	no	yes**
printer	yes	no	yes**
sound	yes	yes	yes
joysticks	yes	yes	yes
graphics	yes	yes	no*

* — output viewed upon returning to 0.9 MHz mode
** — baud rate doubled

NOTES:

1. When the reset button is pushed while in 1.8MHz mode the computer may or may not return to 0.9MHz mode even though the CPU and VDG will still be out of sync.
2. Some of the CPUs produced by Motorolla may not be capable of handling the extra speed so we do not recommend that you use this as a rule.

DISABLE/ENABLE BREAK KEY

It is often handy to disable the BREAK key. Here are two ways of accomplishing it: one is short but can only be entered directly from the keyboard (not from a program), the other can be placed in your programs but is quite a bit longer.

To disable the BREAK key enter the following commands, directly from the keyboard.

```
POKE 411, 228
POKE 412, 203
POKE 413, 4
POKE 414, 237
POKE 415, 228
```

Then to turn the BREAK key on and off use:

POKE 410, 236 to turn it off
POKE 410, 57 to turn it on

Below is a machine language routine which will allow you to turn the BREAK key on and off from you program. To make things easier there is a BASIC program to put this routine into high memory, which you can then save with a CSAVEM "BREAK", &H7FE0, &H7FF$, &H7FE0 to be used with other programs.

```
 10 CLEAR 300, &H7FE0
 20 FOR AD = &H7FE0 TO &H7FF4
 30 READ B$ : B = VAL ("&H" + B$)
 40 POKE AD, B
 50 NEXT AD
 60 POKE &H019B, &H7F : POKE &H019C, &HE0
 70 PRINT "BREAK DISABLED" : POKE &H019A, &H7E
 80 FOR I = 1 TO 2000 : NEXT
 90 PRINT "BREAK ENABLED" : POKE &H019A, &H39
100 FOR I = 1 TO 2000 : NEXT
110 GOTO 70
120 DATA 32,62,1C,AF,BD,80,06,26,07,81,13,26,03
130 DATA 7E,85,2B,97,87,7E,84,A6
```

```
7FE0  32  62    START  LEAS   2,S
7FE2  0C  AF           ANDCC  #$AF
7FE4  BD  8006         JSR    $8006
7FE7  26  07           BNE    :1
7FE9  81  13           CMPA   #$13
7FEB  26  03           BNE    :1
7FED  7E  852B         JMP    $852B
7FF0  97  87    :1     STA    $87
7FF2  7E  84A6         JMP    $84A6
```

SET/RESET FOR SEMIGRAPHIC MODES

This allows the SET/RESET comands to be implemented for semigraphics. First set the mode (see MODE CHANGES) and the appropriate variables. The variables are: X — horizontal co-ordinate; Y — vertical co-ordinate; C — color (1 — 8); SR = 1 — RESET-SET; ST = start of display array.

```
100 IF SR = 0 THEN M = 128 + (C – 1) * 16 : IF (X AND 1) = 0 THEN M
      = M + 10 ELSE M = M + 5
110 IF SR = 1 THEN M = 128 + (C – 1)*16 : IF (X AND 1) = 0 THEN N =
      5 ELSE N = 10
120 AD = ST + Y * 32 + INT(X / 2)
130 IF SR = 0 THEN A = (PEEK (AD) AND 15) : A = A OR M : POKE AD,
      A
140 IF SR = 1 THEN A = (PEEK (AD) AND N) : A = A OR M : POKE AD,
      A
```

AUTO KEY REPEAT

The problem with using the DRAGON keyboard, especially for action type games, is that you cannot tell if someone is holding down one key or if a key is pushed while another is being held down. A very simple way to overcome this is to use the keyboard rollover table located in memory addresses 337 (&H0151) — 345 (&H0159)

ADDRESS		BITS							
DEC	HEX	7	6	5	4	3	2	1	0
337	0151								
338	0152		ENTER	X	P	H	@	8	0
339	0153		CLEAR	Y	Q	I	A	9	1
340	0154			Z	R	J	B	:	2
341	0155			↑	S	K	C	;	3
342	0156			↓	T	L	P	,	4
343	0157			←	U	M	E	—	5
344	0158			→	V	N	F	•	6
345	0159			SPACE	W	O	G	/	7

When there are no keys pressed this table is completely filled with 1's. Whenever a key is pressed its corresponding bit in the table is reset to 0. e.g. when A is pressed bit 2 of memory location 339 (0153hex) is 0. Memory location 337 (0151hex) has the property that if any bit in the same column in the table is 0 then it will be 0. This is the reason that when a key is held down and another pressed then the first released (if both keys are in the same column of the table) the second key does not register as being pressed. To overcome this problem simply POKE 337 with 255 immediately before an INPUT or INKEY$ command.

To allow keys to be repeated when a key is pressed and held down, then each time an INKEY$ call is made the key value is returned, set the entire table to 1's before each INKEY$. For example:

```
10 FOR I = 337 TO 345 : POKE I, 255 : NEXT
20 A$ = INKEY$
30 PRINT A$
40 GOTO 10
```

This program will continue to print the key held down. If you now change line 10 to contain a REM then the program will only print the key once — no matter how long you hold it down.

READING TWO KEYS AT ONCE

Reading two keys pressed simultaneously can be done by reading the keyboard rollover table. When you want to check if a particular key is pressed or not (for action type games) the best way to accomplish this is by POKEing 337 with 255 then PEEKing at the appropriate location and checking to see if the appropriate bit is set or reset. This will tell you if the key is pressed no matter if it has been held down for a while or if any number of other keys are pressed at the time. For example, to check if the up arrow is pressed try this program:

```
10 CLS
20 PRINT @ 0, " "
30 POKE 337, 255
40 IF PEEK(341) AND 32 THEN PRINT "NOT PRESSED" ELSE
PRINT "PRESSED"
50 GOTO 20
```

If line 30 is removed then if two keys in the same column of the rollover table are pressed at the same time then only the first will be recorded in the table.

RECOVERING A PROGRAM AFTER A NEW COMMAND.

After a NEW command has been executed but before any new BASIC lines are added or variables defined the previous program may be restored by the following machine language program.

```
9E     19      LDX     $19
BD     83F3    JSR     #83F3
30     02      LEAX    2,X
9F     1B      STX     $1B
9F     1D      STX     $1D
9F     1F      STX     $1F
37             RTS
```

This program may be entered by the following BASIC program

```
10 CLEAR 200, 32753
20 FOR I = 32754 TO 32767
30 READ X : POKE I, X
40 NEXT I
50 END
60 DATA 158,25,189,131,243,48,2,159,27,159,29,159,31,57
```

After running this program and saving it, type NEW; then LIST, then EXEC 32754, then LIST. If everything was correct your program should be the same as the original program you just entered.

If you have inadvertantly keyed in NEW and you wish to restore your program DO NOT type in the BASIC program above as it will destroy your original program. If you have not CSAVEMed the machine language program then you will have to POKE each number in the DATA statement into its right address (start at 32754 and add 1 for each number POKEd). I recommend that you type in this program now and CSAVEM it, then it can be ready for use whenever you need it (use CSAVEM "UNNEW", 32753, 32767, 32753 and CLOADM whenever you need it) or have this routine at the start of each of your programs.

MERGE

Often it is handy to merge two or more BASIC programs together. For example, you might have a standard sorting routine or a standard menu controller. Merging two programs can be accomplished by the following:

1. CLOAD one of the programs
2. FOR I = 25 TO 28 : PRINT I, PEEK(I)
3. POKE 25, (the number beside 27)
4. POKE 26, (the number beside 28 − 2)
5. Now write down 25 and 26 and numbers beside them
6. CLOAD the second program
7. Make sure all line numbers are greater than those in the first program (see below)
8. POKE 25, (the number you wrote beside 25)
9. POKE 26, (the number you wrote beside 26)

Step 7 (above) is essential otherwise your program line numbers will be out of order and BASIC won't be able to follow them properly so strange things may occur.

There are several ways to ensure that the line numbers are correct.

1. Write all your standard routines with very large numbers (e.g. 10,000 onwards) or small (e.g. less than 100) and write your programs inbetween.
2. After loading in the second program but before the POKEs in steps 8 and 9, RENUMber. At this stage it will only change the line numbers of the second program.

REDEFING BASIC KEYWORDS

By shifting the token table and jump tables out of the ROM into some high RAM locations, resetting the pointers in &H121,122 (token table), &H123,124 (command jump table) and &H126,127 (function jump table) and substituting the addresses of your own command handling routines in the appropriate place of the jump table, you can easily redefine the action to take place when a BASIC keyword is executed.

By taking a careful look at the structure of these tables and expanding them so that their layout is still the same (just bigger) you can even define new BASIC keywords and appropriate actions to take place on their execution.

Below is a small machine language routine which redefines the SOUND command (this could use the machine language program in the sound chapter (4)).

```
7000  108E  7D9F  START  LDY   #$7D9F
7004    8E  8033         LDX   #$8033
7007  10BF  0121         STY   $0121
700B    A6  80     LOOP  LDA   ,X+
700D    A7  C0           STA   ,Y+
700F    8C  8293         CMPX  #$829B
7012    2D  F7           BLT   LOOP
7014    8E  7EC0         LDX   #$7EC0
7017    BF  0123         STX   $0123
701A    8E  7F36         LDX   #$7F36
701D    BF  0126         STX   #$0126
7020    8E  7FBC         LDX   #$7FBC
7023    BF  0128         STX   $0128
7026    8E  ?*           LDX   "START OF SOUND ROUTINE"
7029    BF  7E8C         STX   $7E8C
702C    39               RTS
```

* Depends on where you load your sound routine

BOXES SHOWING PAGE SWAPPING

This program, although not very useful, shows just how fast pages of screen can be swapped to make fast animation.

```
10 PCLEAR 8
20 FOR PD=1TO8
30 PMODE 0,PD
40 PCLS
50 SCREEN0,0
60 LINE(128-11*PD,96-11*PD)-(128+11
   *PD,96+11*PD),PSET,B
70 NEXT PD
80 I=1:SP=1
90 I=I+SP
100 IF I<=1 OR I=>8 THEN SP=-SP
110 PMODE0,I
120 SCREEN1,0
130 GOTO 90
```

VARIOUS CIRCLES

This program shows the power of the CIRCLE command and produces some quite nice pictures.

```
0 '** MAIN PROGRAM **'
10 CLS
20 PRINT@42,"CIRCLES"
30 PRINT@98,"r - RANDOM"
40 PRINT@162,"f - FILL OWN OPTIONS"
50 PRINT@226,"g - PIE GRAPH"
60 PRINT@290,"p - 'PACMAN'"
70 PRINT@354,"a - A FACE"
80 PRINT@450,"PRESS ONE OF THE ABOVE KEYS"
90 PRINT@482,"enter TO RETURN TO THE MENU";
100 A$=INKEY$:IF A$="" THEN 100
110 A=INSTR("RFGPA",A$)
120 IF A=0 THEN 100
130 PMODE3,1:PCLS:SCREEN1,0
140 ON A GOSUB 200,300,400,500,600
150 GOTO10
199 '** RANOM CIRCLES **'
200 PCLS
210 CIRCLE(RND(250),RND(180)),RND(70),0,RND(4)
220 FORI=1TO200:NEXTI
```

```
230 A$=INKEY$:IFA$="" THEN 200
240 IF ASC(A$)=13 THEN RETURN ELSE 200
299 '** OWN OPTIONS **'
300 CLS
310 INPUT"CO-ORDINATES(X,Y)";X,Y
320 INPUT"RADIUS";R
330 INPUT"COLOR(0-7)";C
340 INPUT"HEIGHT-WIDTH RATIO(0-4)";HW
350 INPUT"START(0-1)";S
360 INPUT"END(0-1)";E
370 PMODE3,1:PCLS:SCREEN1,0
380 CIRCLE(X,Y),R,C,HW,S,E
390 A$=INKEY$:IF A$="" THEN 390
395 IF ASC(A$)=13 THEN RETURN ELSE 390
399 '** PIE GRAPH **'
400 CIRCLE(118,106),60,0,1,0,.75
410 CIRCLE(138,86),60,0,1,.75,1
420 LINE(118,106)-(118,46),PSET
430 LINE(118,106)-(178,106),PSET
440 LINE(138,86)-(138,26),PSET
450 LINE(138,86)-(198,86),PSET
460 PAINT(149,75),0,0
470 A$=INKEY$:IF A$="" THEN 470
480 IF ASC(A$)=13 THEN RETURN ELSE 470
499 '** PACK MAN **
500 CIRCLE(128,96),80,0,1,.06,.94
510 CIRCLE(148,50),9,0
520 LINE(128,96)-(200,65),PSET
530 LINE(128,96)-(200,119),PSET
540 PAINT(120,20),0,0
550 A$=INKEY$:IF A$="" THEN 550
560 IF ASC(A$)=13 THEN RETURN ELSE 550
599 '** A FACE **
600 CIRCLE(128,96),70,0,1.2
610 CIRCLE(50,96),10,0,3
620 CIRCLE(207,96),10,0,3
630 CIRCLE(100,70),12,0,.7
640 CIRCLE(156,70),12,0,.7
650 CIRCLE(128,96),6,0,3
660 CIRCLE(128,130),45,0,.7,0,.5
670 CIRCLE(128,130),47,0,.25,0,.5
```

```
680 PAINT(128,150),0,0
690 A$=INKEY$:IF A$="" THEN 690
700 IF ASC(A$)=13 THEN RETURN ELSE 690
```

LINES

This program, like the last few, is not particularly useful but demonstrates the power of the graphics and produces some interesting effects.

```
10 CLS
20 PMODE4,1:PCLS
30 PI=3.141592654
40 R=180/PI
50 SX=192/42767
60 SY=255/42767
70 INPUT"STEP SIZE";I
80 IF I=0 THEN END
90 PCLS:SCREEN1,1
100 A1=128:B1=96
110 A2=128:B2=96
120 FORK=1 TO 16000 STEP I
130 I=K/R
140 A=K*COS(I)*SY+A2
150 B=K*SIN(I)*SX+B2
160 LINE(A,B)-(A1,B1),PSET
170 A1=A:B1=B
180 NEXTK
190 A$=INKEY$:IFA$=""THEN190
200 GOTO70
```

SCROLLS

Here are some machine language programs to scroll the text screen.

```
7000    C6  01      LEFT    LDB   #01
7002    8E  0400    :1      LDX   #$400
7005    A6  85      :2      LDA   B,X
7007    5A                  DECB
7008    A7  85              STA   B,X
700A    5C                  INCB
700B    30  88 20           LEAX  32,X
700E    8C  0600            CMPX  #$600
7011    2D  F2              BLT   :2
7013    5C                  INCB
```

```
7014    C1  1F                  CMPB  #31
7016    2F  EA                  BLE   :1
7018    39                      RTS

7019    C6  1E       RIGHT      LDB   #30
701B    8E  0400     :1         LDX   #$400
701E    A6  85       :2         LDA   B,X
7020    5C                      INCB
7021    A7  85                  STA   B,X
7023    5A                      DECB
7024    30  88 20               LEAX  32,X
7027    8C  0600                CMPX  #$600
702A    2D  F2                  BLT   :2
702C    5A                      DECB
702D    C1  FF                  CMPB  #$FF
702F    26  EA                  BNE   :1
7031    39                      RTS

7032    8E  0400     UP         LDX   #$400
7035  10AE  88 20    :1         LDY   32,X
7039  10AF  81                  STY   ,X++
703C    8C  0600                CMPX  #$600
703F    2D  F4                  BLT   :1
7041    39                      RTS

7042    8E  05E2     DOWN       LDX   #$5E2
7045  10AE  83       :1         LDY   ,--X
7048  10AF  88 20               STY   32,X
704C    8C  0400                CMPX  #$400
704F    2E  F4                  BGT   :1
7051    39                      RTS
```

NOTE: These scroll routines leave the last line to be scrolled (e.g. right: the far left column, up: bottom line) untouched. This means that repeated calls to these routines will fill up the screen with the last line.

To use these routines in a game for scrolling; as soon as these routines have finished then fill in that last line with the new information to go on the screen.

To use these routines on the graphics screens the starting and ending addresses need to be changed as well as the 'gap' between each line. On the text screen the 'gap' is 32, the start address &H400 and end address &H600.

MOVEMENT

There are two main ways to produce movement from BASIC. The combination of the GET and PUT commands and writing-overwriting-writing. The second method is okay if the object being moved is not very complicated, just a few lines, but would be too slow for complicated Hi Res graphics. Using GET/PUT can move quite complicated graphics very quickly. An example of just how fast this is is given below:

```
10 PMODE4,1
20 SCREEN1,0
30 PCLS
40 DIM V(0,3)
50 SP=1:I=0
60 CIRCLE(20,20),3
80 GET(15,15)-(25,25),V,G
90 PUT(15+I,15+I)-(25+I,25+I),V,PSET
100 I=I+SP
110 IF I>150 OR I<0 THEN SP=-SP*1.1
120 GOTO90
```

After each 'bounce' the circle moves faster and as it moves faster becomes jerky. If it is left running long enough, the new circle does not erase all of the previous ones leaving 'shadows' behind.

SOUND IN MACHINE LANGUAGE

This machine language program uses the single-bit-sound (bit 1) in the &HFF22 PIA register. There are three main routines; the first, START, sets up the PIA chip ready for use by the other routines; the second, CONTROL, handles the control of the sound; the third, SOUND, produces the actual note.

The CONTROL routine takes four 16-bit numbers (which it assumes start at &H7100) to control the sound. These numbers have the following effect: the first, START, is the frequency at which to start; the second, STOP, is the frequency at which to stop; the third, INCR, is the amount to increment frequencies by between each note and the fourth, DURA, is the length of time to play each note before moving on to the next. These four numbers form a phrase and phrases are repeated, until a phrase with a zero increment value is encountered.

Note that frequencies are back-to-front as the smaller the number the higher the frequency, and because of this style of sound production, the higher the frequency the shorter the note for the same duration value.

Below is an assembler listing followed by a BASIC program which will load in the machine language program and prompt for phrases, and will play these phrases when a terminating one is encountered.
Note that the start frequency value is destroyed during the running of the program but all others are preserved.

```
7000                                ORG     $7000
7000  34    76    START             PSHS    D,X,Y,U
7002  B6    FF23                    LDA     $FF23
7005  84    F3                      ANDA    #$F3
7007  B7    FF23                    STA     $FF23
700A  F6    FF22                    LDB     $FF22
700D  CA    02                      ORB     #$02
700F  F7    FF22                    STB     $FF22
7012  8A    04                      ORA     #$04
7014  B7    FF23                    STA     $FF23
7017  8D    03                      BRS     CONTROL
7019  35    76                      PULS    D,X,Y,U
701B  39                            RTS
701C  CE    70F8  CONTROL           LDU     #$70F8
701F  33    48    NEXT              LEAU    8,U
7021  AE    44                      LDX     4,U
7023  27    26                      BEQ     RETURN
7025  AE    C4                      LDX     ,U
7027  AC    42                      CMPX    2,U
7029  27    F4                      BEQ     NEXT
702B  2C    0F                      BGE     BIGGER
702D  8D    1D    SMALLER           BSR     SOUND
702F  EC    C4                      LDD     ,U
7031  E3    44                      ADDD    4,U
7033  10A3  42                      CMPD    2,U
7036  2C    E7                      BGE     NEXT
7038  ED    C4                      STD     ,U
703A  20    F1                      BRA     SMALLER
703C  8D    0E    BIGGER            BSR     SOUND
703E  EC    C4                      LDD     ,U
7040  A3    44                      SUBD    4,U
7042  10A3  42                      CMPD    2,U
7045  2F    D8                      BLE     NEXT
7047  ED    C4                      STD     ,U
7049  20    F1                      BRA     BIGGER
704B  39          RETURN            RTS
704C  AE    46    SOUND             LDX     6,U
704E  10AE  C4    :1                LDY     ,U
7051  31    3F    :2                LEAY    −1,Y
7053  26    FC                      BNE     :2
7055  B6    FF22                    LDA     $FF22
```

```
7058    88    02          EORA    #$02
705A    B7    FF22        STA     $FF22
705D    30    1F          LEAX    -1,X
705F    26    ED          BNE     :1
7061    39                RTS
```

The BASIC program below loads the machine language program in, sets up its parameters, then runs the routine.
It asks:
NEW PHRASE: If you answer Y then you can define a new lot of parameters.
If you answer N then the set previously defined is used.
The Parameters: These are all 4 digit numbers so you must include leading zeros to make them 4 digits long.
MORE: If you answer Y then you are asked 'NEW PHRASE?' and the processing continues.
If you answer N then the current phrase is played and you are asked 'NEW PHRASE?' etc.
Here are some examples to get you going.

Start Frequency	0400
End Frequency	0000
Increment	0001
Duration	0010

Start Frequency	0400	0300
End Frequency	0300	0600
Increment	0001	0001
Duration	0080	0010

Start Frequency	0200	0400	0400
End Frequency	0400	0400	0000
Increment	0010	0001	0005
Duration	0010	0090	0010

```
10 CLEAR 200,&H6FFF
20 AD=&H7100
30 FORI=&H7000 TO &H7061
40 READ X$:X=VAL("&H"+X$):POKE I,X
50 CSUM=CSUM+X
60 NEXTI
70 IF CSUM<>12446 THEN PRINT "DATA ERROR",CSUM:END
80 CLS:PRINT " ** SOUND PHRASES **"
90 PRINT "NEW PHRASE ?"
100 A$=INKEY$:IF A$="" THEN 100
110 IF A$="N" THEN 230 ELSE IF A$<>"Y" THEN 100
120 INPUT "STARTING FREQUENCY";PR$(0)
130 IF LEN(PR$(0))<>4 THEN 120
140 INPUT "ENDING FREQUENCY";PR$(1)
150 IF LEN(PR$(1))<>4 THEN 140
160 INPUT "INCREMENT";PR$(2)
170 IF LEN(PR$(2))<>4 THEN 160
180 INPUT "DURATION";PR$(3)
190 IF LEN(PR$(3))<>4 THEN 180
200 PR$(3)=STR$(VAL(PR$(3))/10)
210 PR$(3)=MID$(PR$(3),2)
220 IF LEN(PR$(3))<4 THEN PR$(3)="0" + PR$(3):GOTO 220
230 FORI=0TO3
240 POKE AD+(2*I),VAL(LEFT$(PR$(I),2))
250 POKE AD+(2*I)+1,VAL(RIGHT$(PR$(I),2))
260 NEXTI
270 AD=AD+8
280 PRINT "MORE ?"
290 A$=INKEY$:IF A$="" THEN290
300 IF A$="Y" THEN 80 ELSE IF A$<>"N" THEN 290
310 POKE AD+4,0:POKE AD+5,0
320 EXEC &H7000
330 GOTO 80
340 END
350 DATA 34,76,B6,FF,23,84,F3,B7,FF,23,F6,FF,22
360 DATA CA,02,F7,FF,22,8A,04,B7,FF,23,8D,03,35,76
370 DATA 39,CE,70,F8,33,48,AE,44,27,26,AE,C4,AC,
    42,27,F4
380 DATA 2C,0F,8D,1D,EC,C4,E3,44,10,A3,42,2C,E7
390 DATA ED,C4,20,F1,8D,0E,EC,C4,A3,44,10,A3,42
400 DATA 2F,D8,ED,C4,20,F1,39,AE,46,10,AE,C4,31,
    3F,26,FC,B6,FF,22
410 DATA 88,02,B7,FF,22,30,1F,26,ED,39
```

CHARACTERS IN HI-RES GRAPHICS

Most characters on computers are defined by dots. This means that although BASIC does not allow text on the hi res screens, you can define and print your own.

The first thing to do is define your characters. Use graph paper or draw up your own grids. When 5x7 dot-matrix characters are used (example below), there is room for 42 characters accross and 24 down, allowing for a separation space of 1 pixel between characters. Larger matrices 6x8 give better resolution but less characters on the screen.

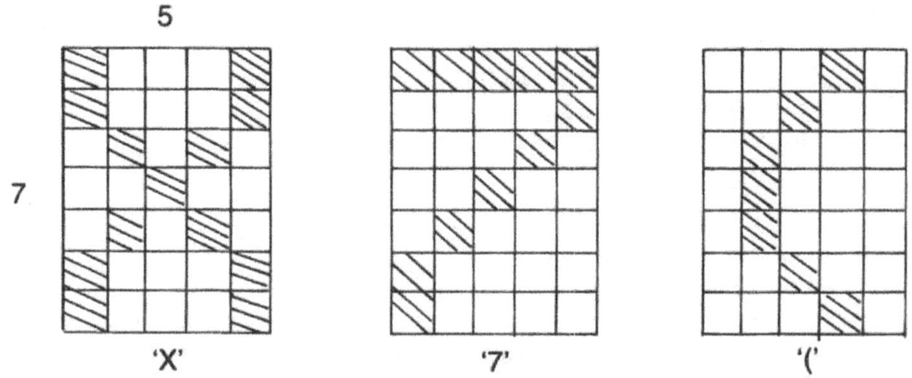

Once you have designed your characters, the problem is to hold them in memory and display them on the screen. If you are using BASIC there are two main methods to accomplish this.

One is to use the DRAW command. Here is an example of how to use DRAW to produce characters.

```
DRAW "L6R4D8U8R4" : REM T
DRAW "D8U4R6D4U8" : REM H
DRAW "D8R6BU4L6U4R6 : REM E
DRAW "D8R4E2U4H2L4BR6" : REM D
```

The other way is to hold your characters in an array and use GET to store them and PUT to display them on the screen. Most computers use an 8x8 grid for their character block as this gives a fair trade-off between readability and the number of characters that can fit on the screen. Also, using 8 pixels accross the character allows 8 bytes to hold 1 character without any wasteage. In the hi res modes this gives you 32 characters by 24 lines on the screen.

The first step to defining your own character set is as above and if using the 8x8 grid you should leave a one-bit-buffer on one side of the character and either on the top or the bottom of the character. The usual way is to leave the bottom line and the right line free. In effect his gives you a 7x7 area for your character.

After drawing all your characters up on graph paper it is time to enter and store them in the computer. This can be done by PSETting the appropriate points on the screen to build up the character, then GETting that character off the screen and into an array. The array must be of DIM (0,2) for an 8x8 character grid. This means there is plenty of room in memory for a complete 96 upper and lower case ASCII character set.

APPENDIX A

TABLES

BASIC KEYWORDS

WORD	DESCRIPTION
ABS	Absolute function
AND	Logical operator
ASC	Function to return ASCII codes
ATN	Arctangent function
AUDIO	Switch cassette-to-TV on and off
CHR$	Function to return characters from ASCII codes
CIRCLE	Draw a circle on a graphic screen
CLEAR	Initialize variables and reserve memory
CLOAD	Load a BASIC program from tape
CLOADM	Load a machine code program from tape
CLOSE	Close open files or devices
CLS	Clear display to specified color
COLOR	Set foreground and background colours
CONT	Restart program execution
COS	Cosine function
CSAVE	Save BASIC programs on tape
CSAVEM	Save machine code programs on tape
DATA	Store data inside programs
DEF FN	Define numeric function
DEFUSR	Define entry point for machine code routine
DEL	Delete BASIC program lines
DIM	Define array dimensions
DRAW	Draw lines on a grahics screen
EDIT	Change program lines
ELSE	Options with IF statements
END	End a program
EOF	Returns whether a file is at the end or not
EXEC	Transfer control to a machine code program
EXP	Natural Exponentiation of a number
FIX	Truncates real numbers to give integers
FOR/TO/STEP/NEXT	Control a loop with a control varaible
GET	Store a rectangle of graphics screen into an array
GOSUB	Transfer execution to a subroutine
GOTO	Transfer execution to the specified line
HEX$	Computes hexadecimal values
IF/THEN/ELSE	Test relationships
INKEY$	Return last key pressed
INPUT	Accept data from keyboard
INPUT#−1	Accept data from tape
INSTR	String search function
INT	Converts number to integer
JOYSTK	Sample joystick ports
LEFT$	Returns left portion of string
LEN	Returns the number of characters in a string
LET	Assignment statement option
LIST	List specified lines on screen

LLIST	List specified lines on line printer
LINE	Draws a line on a graphic page
LINE INPUT	Accepts a complete line from keyboard
LOG	Returns the natural logarithm
MEM	Returns the amount of free memory
MID$	Returns or assigns a substring in a larger string
MOTOR	Turns the tape motor on and off
NEW	Erases BASIC program
NEXT	End of FOR loop
ON...GOSUB	Multi-branch to subroutines
ON...GOTO	Multi-branch to line numbers
OPEN	Prepares files or devices for use
PAINT	Paints a portion of a graphic screen
PCLEAR	Reserves memory for graphic pages
PCLS	Clears a graphic page
PCOPY	Copies one graphic page to another
PEEK	Returns the contents of a memory location
PLAY	Plays music
PMODE	Specifies resolution and starting page of graphics
POINT	Returns attributes of a character cell
POKE	Sets a memory location to a specified value
POS	Returns current cursor position
PPOINT	Returns atttributes of a cell on a graphics page
PRESET	Sets a cell to background color
PRINT	Puts a message on the screen
PRINT#-1	Puts data on tape
PRINT#-2	Prints on the line printer
PRINT TAB	Moves cursor to specified column before printing
PRINT USING	Prints data in the specified format
PRINT @	Starts printing at the specified position on screen
PSET	Sets point to specified colour
PUT	Displays graphic data from an array on a graphics screen
READ	Reads data from the DATA statements
REM	Allows insertion of comments
RENUM	Renumbers the lines of a BASIC program
RESET	Set specified cell to background color
RESTORE	Set pointer to first item of DATA statements
RETURN	Returns control after a subroutine call
RIGHT$	Returns the right portion of a string
RND	Returns random numbers
RUN	Executes a BASIC program
SCREEN	Specifies type of screen and colour set
SET	Set a dot on screen to the specified colour
SGN	Returns the sign of a number
SKIPF	Skips a file on tape
SIN	Sine function
SOUND	Plays a sound
STEP	Option for FOR loops
STOP	Stops execution of a BASIC program
STRING$	Build a string of characters
STR$	Convert a number to a string
SQR	Returns square root of a number
TAN	Tangent function
TIMER	Returns contents of, or sets, the timer
TO	Part of the FOR loop
TROFF	Turn off program tracer
TRON	Turn on program tracer

USR	Calls machine language routine
VAL	Converts a string to a number
VARPTR	Returns the start address of a BASIC variable

BASIC SYMBOLS

SYMBOL	PURPOSE
+	Addition of numbers and strings; sharp of a note in PLAY
−	Subtraction; flat of a note in PLAY; minus print in USING
*	Multiplication
/	Division
=	Equals
>	Greater than
<	Less than
>= or =>	Greater than or equal to
<= or =<	Less then or equal to
<> or ><	Not equal to
'	Abbreviation of REM
?	Abbreviation of PRINT
"	Denotes a string constant
:	Separates multiple BASICstatements on the same line
↑	Raises numbers to powers, eg. 3 ↑ 5 = 3^5

SPECIAL KEYBOARD KEYS

KEY	PURPOSE
←	Backspace cursor and erase last entry
ENTER	Tell computer end of data input has been reached
BREAK	Stops program execution
SHIFT @	Pause program execution (any key to continue)
CLEAR	Clears the screen

APPENDIX B

ERROR MESSAGES

MESSAGE	EXPLANATION
/0	Division by zero
A0	Attempting to open a file which is already open
BS	Bad Subscript. Trying to use an array subscript outside the range it was defined as. Sometimes if a computer cannot recognize a function this message is given.
CN	Can't Continue. When you use the CONT command after making changes to the program or the program is at the end.
DD	Trying to dimension the same array more than once.
DN	Device number error. There are only three device numbers. −0 — standard, screen, keyboard; −1 — tape; −2 — printer.
DS	Direct Statement. This occurs if a direct statement is in a data file on tape.
FC	Illegal Function Call. This occurs when a function or statement parameter is out of range.
FD	Bad File Data.This occurs when the wrong type of data is being read from a file, that is if numeric data is being INPUT into a string variable and vice-versa.
FM	Bad File Mode. This occurs when you try to INPUT data from a file OPEN for OUTPUT or vice-versa.
ID	Illegal Direct Statement. For example, when an INPUT statement is executed outside a program.
IE	Input Past End of File. Use EOF to check for the end of the file.
IO	Input/Output Error. Often caused by bad tapes, i.e. when the DRAGON cannot understand what is on the tape.
LS	String too Long. A string can only have 255 characters in it.
NF	NEXT without FOR. Occurs when a NEXT statement is encountered without a corresponding FOR statement.
NO	File Not Open. You cannot access a data file without first opening it.
OD	Out of Data. When a READ statement is executed and there are no elements left in any DATA statements.

OM	Out of Memory. All available memory has been used or reserved.
OS	Out of String Space. There is not enough space for string operations. You may be able to CLEAR more space.
OV	Overflow. A number has been made too long for the computer to store. The range of numbers available is +1.7E+38.
RG	RETURN without GOSUB. A RETURN statement has be encountered without a previous GOSUB statement.
SN	Syntax Error. This message is given whenever the DRAGON cannot understand the command. May result from misspelling the word or incorrect number of parameters, etc.
ST	String formula too complex.Break up the formula into shorter steps.
TM	Type Mismatch. This occurs when numeric data is assigned to a string variable (e.g. A$ = 8) or vice-versa.
UL	Undefined Line Number. This happens when any command references a line number which does not exist.

APPENDIX C

MEMORY MAP

DECIMAL ADDRESS	CONTENTS	HEX ADDRESS
0 — 1023	System Work Area	0 — 3FF
1024 — 1535	Text Screen	400 — 5FF
1536 — 3071	Graphic — page 1	600 — BFF
3072 — 4607	Graphic — page 2	C00 — 11FF
4608 — 6143	Graphic — page 3	1200 — 17FF
6144 — 7679	Graphic — page 4	1800 — 1DFF
7680 — 9215	Graphic — page 5	1E00 — 23FF
9216 — 10751	Graphic — page 6	2400 — 29FF
10752 — 12287	Graphic — page 7	2A00 — 2FFF
12288 — 13823	Graphic — page 8	3000 — 35FF
13824 — 32767	Program and Variables — user's	3600 — 7FFF
32768 — 49151	BASIC ROM	8000 — BFFF
49152 — 65279	Cartridge Port	C000 — FEFF
65280 — 65535	Input/Output	FF00 — FFFF

APPENDIX D

COLOUR CODES

These are codes for each of the nine colours you can create

Code	Color
0	Black
1	Green
2	Yellow
3	Blue
4	Red
5	Buff
6	Cyan
7	Magenta
8	Orange

The colour may vary in shade from these, depending on your TV. Colour 0 (Black) is actually an absence of colour.

COLOUR-SET TABLE

PMODE #	Color Set	Two Color Combination	Four Color Combination
4	0	Black/Green	—
	1	Black/Buff	—
3	0	—	Green/Yellow/Blue/Red
	1	—	Buff/Cyan/Magenta/Orange
2	0	Black/Green	—
	1	Black/Buff	—
1	0	—	Green/Yellow/Blue/Red
	1	—	Buff/Cyan/Magenta/Orange
0	0	Black/Green	—
	1	Black/Buff	—

APPENDIX E

CHARACTER CODES

For use with CHR$ function and ASC function.

HEX	DEC	20 32	30 48	40 64	50 80	60 96	70 112
0	0		0	@	P	@	P
1	1	!	1	A	Q	A	Q
2	2	"	2	B	R	B	R
3	3	#	3	C	S	C	S
4	4	$	4	D	T	D	T
5	5	%	5	E	U	E	U
6	6	8	6	F	V	F	V
7	7	'	7	G	W	G	W
8	8	(	8	H	X	H	X
9	9	)	9	I	Y	I	Y
A	10	*	:	J	Z	J	Z
B	11	+	;	K	[	K	[
C	12	,	÷	L	÷	L	÷
D	13	—	=	M	]	M	]
E	14	•	÷	N	÷	N	÷
F	15	/	?	O	—	O	—

NOTE:

1) The last two columns are the lower case values of the previous two columns and will be shown as inverse video on the screen.

2) Characters 0—31 are ASCII control characters and have no effect on screen. Two exceptions are 8 which is backspace and 13 which is carriage return.

APPENDIX F

PRINT @ GRID

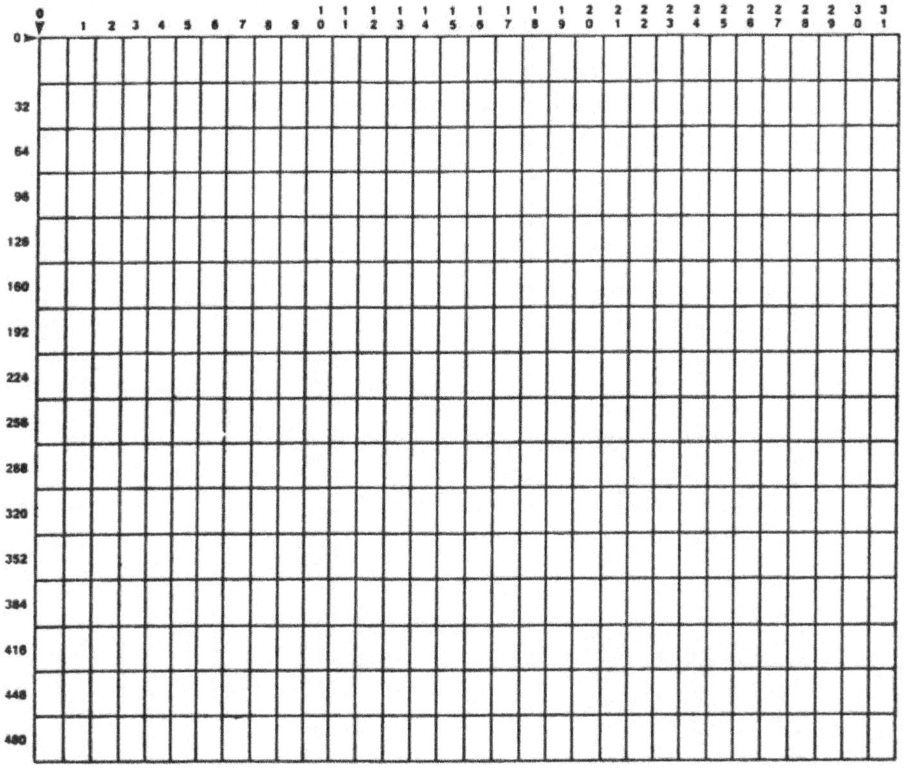

APPENDIX G

ASCII CODES FOR KEYS

Key	Hex #		Decimal #	
	Unshifted	Shifted	Unshifted	Shifted
BREAK	03	03	03	03
CLEAR	0C	—	12	—
ENTER	0D	0D	13	13
SPACEBAR	20	—	32	32
!	—	21	33	—
"	—	22	34	—
#	—	23	35	—
$	—	24	36	—
%	—	25	37	—
&	—	26	38	—
'	—	27	39	—
(	—	28	40	—
)	—	29	41	—
*	—	2A	42	—
+	—	2B	43	—
–	2D	—	45	—
.	2E	—	46	—
/	2F	—	47	—
0	30	—	48	
1	31	—	49	—
2	32	—	50	—
3	33	—	51	—
4	34	—	52	—
5	35	—	53	—
6	36	—	54	—
7	37	—	55	—
8	38	—	56	—
9	39	—	57	—
:	3A	—	58	—
;	3B	—	59	—
<	3C	—	60	—
=	3D	—	61	—
>	3E	—	62	—
?	3F	—	63	—
@	40	13	64	19
A	61	41	97	65
B	62	42	98	66
C	63	43	99	67
D	64	44	100	68
E	65	45	101	69
F	66	46	102	70
G	67	47	103	71
H	68	48	104	72
I	69	49	105	73
J	6A	4A	106	74
K	6B	4B	107	75
L	6C	4C	108	76
M	6D	4D	109	77

Key	Hex #		Decimal #	
	Unshifted	Shifted	Unshifted	Shifted
N	6E	4E	110	78
O	6F	4F	111	79
P	70	50	112	80
Q	71	51	113	81
R	72	52	114	82
S	73	53	115	83
T	74	54	116	84
U	75	55	117	85
V	76	56	118	86
W	77	57	119	87
X	78	58	120	88
Y	79	59	121	89
Z	7A	5A	122	90
↑	5E	5F	94	95
↓	OA	5B	10	91
←	O8	15	8	21
→	O9	5D	9	93

Note: For characters A through Z, press the key combination of SHIFT 0 to utilize the upper/lowercase option. The unshifted codes will then apply.

APPENDIX H

CHARACTER CODES

For use with PEEKs and POKEs direct to the text screen.

HEX		0	10	20	30	40	50	60	70
	DEC	0	16	32	48	64	80	96	112
0	0	@	P		0	@	P		0
1	1	A	Q	!	1	A	Q	!	1
2	2	B	R	"	2	B	R	"	2
3	3	C	S	#	3	C	S	#	3
4	4	D	T	$	4	D	T	$	4
5	5	E	U	%	5	E	U	%	5
6	6	F	V	8	6	F	V	8	6
7	7	G	W	'	7	G	W	'	7
8	8	H	X	(	8	H	X	(	8
9	9	I	Y	)	9	I	Y	)	9
A	10	J	Z	*	:	J	Z	*	:
B	11	K	[	+	;	K	[	+	;
C	12	L	÷	,	÷	L	÷	,	÷
D	13	M	]	—	=	M	]	—	=
E	14	N	÷	•	÷	N	÷	•	÷
F	15	O	—	/	?	O	—	/	?

APPENDIX I

BASE CONVERSIONS

The following table lists base conversions for all one-byte values.

DEC.	BINARY	HEX.	OCT.
0	00000000	00	000
1	00000001	01	001
2	00000010	02	002
3	00000011	03	003
4	00000100	04	004
5	00000101	05	005
6	00000110	06	006
7	00000111	07	007
8	00001000	08	010
9	00001001	09	011
10	00001010	0A	012
11	00001011	0B	013
12	00001100	0C	014
13	00001101	0D	015
14	00001110	0E	016
15	00001111	0F	017
16	00010000	10	020
17	00010001	11	021
18	00010010	12	022
19	00010011	13	023
20	00010100	14	024
21	00010101	15	025
22	00010110	16	026
23	00010111	17	027
24	00011000	18	030
25	00011001	19	031
26	00011010	1A	032
27	00011011	1B	033
28	00011100	1C	034
29	00011101	1D	035
30	00011110	1E	036
31	00011111	1F	037
32	00100000	20	040
33	00100001	21	041
34	00100010	22	042
35	00100011	23	043
36	00100100	24	044
37	00100101	25	045
38	00100110	26	046
39	00100111	27	047
40	00101000	28	050
41	00101001	29	051
42	00101010	2A	052
43	00101011	2B	053
44	00101100	2C	054
45	00101101	2D	055
46	00101110	2E	056
47	00101111	2F	057
48	00110000	30	060
49	00110001	31	061
50	00110010	32	062
51	00110011	33	063
52	00110100	34	064
53	00110101	35	065
54	00110110	36	066
55	00110111	37	067
56	00111000	38	070
57	00111001	39	071
58	00111010	3A	072
59	00111011	3B	073

DEC.	BINARY	HEX.	OCT.
60	00111100	3C	074
61	00111101	3D	075
62	00111110	3E	076
63	00111111	3F	077
64	01000000	40	100
65	01000001	41	101
66	01000010	42	102
67	01000011	43	103
68	01000100	44	104
69	01000101	45	105
70	01000110	46	1060
71	01000111	47	107
72	01001000	48	110
73	01001001	49	111
74	01001010	4A	112
75	01001011	4B	113
76	01001100	4C	114
77	01001101	4D	115
78	01001110	4E	116
79	01001111	4F	117
80	01010000	50	120
81	01010001	51	121
82	01010010	52	122
83	01010011	53	123
84	01010100	54	124
85	01010101	55	125
86	01010110	56	126
87	01010111	57	127
88	01011000	58	130
89	01011001	59	131
90	01011010	5A	132
91	01011011	5B	133
92	01011100	5C	134
93	01011101	5D	135

DEC.	BINARY	HEX.	OCT.
94	01011110	5E	136
95	01011111	5F	137
96	01100000	60	140
97	01100001	61	141
98	01100010	62	142
99	01100011	63	143
100	01100100	64	144
101	01100101	65	145
102	01100110	66	146
103	01100111	67	147
104	01101000	68	150
105	01101001	69	151
106	01101010	6A	152
107	01101011	6B	153
108	01101100	6c	154
109	01101101	6D	1550
110	01101110	6E	156
111	01101111	6F	157
112	01110000	70	160
113	01110001	71	161
114	01110010	72	162
115	01110011	73	163
116	01110100	74	164
117	01110101	75	165
118	01110110	76	166
119	01110111	77	167
120	01111000	78	170
121	01111001	79	171
122	01111010	7A	172
123	01111011	7B	173
124	01111100	7C	174
125	01111101	7D	175
126	01111110	7E	176
127	01111111	7F	177

DEC.	BINARY	HEX.	OCT.
128	10000000	80	200
129	10000001	81	201
130	10000010	82	202
131	10000011	83	203
132	10000100	84	204
133	10000101	85	205
134	10000110	86	206
135	10000111	87	207
136	10001000	88	210
137	10001001	89	211
138	10001010	8A	212
139	10001011	8B	213
140	10001100	8C	214
141	10001101	8D	215
142	10001110	8E	216
143	10001111	8F	217
144	10010000	90	220
145	10010001	91	221
146	10010010	92	222
147	10010011	93	223
148	10010100	94	224
149	10010101	95	255
150	10010110	96	226
151	10010111	97	227
152	10011000	98	230
153	10011001	99	231
154	10011010	9A	232
155	10011011	9B	233
156	10011100	9C	234
157	10011101	9D	235
158	10011110	9E	236
159	10011111	9F	237
160	10100000	A0	240
161	10100001	A1	241

DEC.	BINARY	HEX.	OCT.
162	10100010	A2	242
163	10100011	A3	243
164	10100100	A4	244
165	10100101	A5	245
166	10100110	A6	246
167	10100111	A7	247
168	10101000	A8	250
169	10101001	A9	251
170	10101010	AA	252
171	10101011	AB	253
172	10101100	AC	254
173	10101101	AD	255
174	10101110	AE	256
175	10101111	AF	257
176	10110000	B0	260
177	10110001	B1	261
178	10110010	B2	262
179	10110011	B3	263
180	10110100	B4	264
181	10110101	B5	265
182	10110110	B6	266
183	10110111	B7	267
184	10111000	B8	270
185	10111001	B9	271
186	10111010	BA	272
187	10111011	BB	273
188	10111100	BC	274
189	10111101	BD	275
190	10111110	BE	276
191	10111111	BF	277
192	11000000	C0	300
193	11000001	C1	301
194	11000010	C2	302
195	11000011	C3	303

DEC.	BINARY	HEX.	OCT.
196	11000100	C4	304
197	11000101	C5	305
198	11000110	C6	306
199	11000111	C7	307
200	11001000	C8	310
201	11001001	C9	311
202	11001010	CA	312
203	11001011	CB	313
204	11001100	CC	314
205	11001101	CD	315
206	11001110	CE	316
207	11001111	CF	317
208	11010000	D0	320
209	11010001	D1	321
210	11010010	D2	322
211	11010011	D3	323
212	11010100	D4	324
213	11010101	D5	325
214	11010110	D6	326
215	11010111	D7	327
216	11011000	D8	330
217	11011001	D9	331
218	11011010	DA	332
219	11011011	DB	333
220	11011100	DC	334
221	11011101	DD	335
222	11011110	DE	336
223	11011111	DF	337
224	11100000	E0	340
225	11100001	E1	341
226	11100010	E2	342

DEC.	BINARY	HEX.	OCT.
227	11100011	E3	343
228	11100100	E4	344
229	11100101	E5	345
230	11100110	E6	346
231	11100111	E7	347
232	11101000	E8	350
233	11101001	E9	351
234	11101010	EA	352
235	11101011	EB	353
236	11101100	EC	354
237	11101101	ED	355
238	11101110	EE	356
239	11101111	EF	357
240	11110000	F0	360
241	11110001	F1	361
242	11110010	F2	362
243	11110011	F3	363
244	11110100	F4	364
245	11110101	F5	365
246	11110110	F6	366
247	11110111	F7	367
248	11111000	F8	370
249	11111001	F9	371
250	11111010	FA	372
251	11111011	FB	373
252	11111100	FC	374
253	11111101	FD	375
254	11111110	FE	376
255	11111111	FF	377

APPENDIX J

OP	MNEM	MODE	~	#	OP	MNEM	MODE	~	#	OP	MNEM	MODE	~	#
00	NEG	DIRECT	6	2	1C	ANDCC	IMMED	3	2	2E	BGT	RELATIVE	3	2
03	COM		6	2	1D	SEX	INHERENT	2	1	2F	BLE	RELATIVE	3	2
04	LSR		6	2	1E	EXG		8	2	30	LEAX	INDEXED	4	2
06	ROR		6	2	1F	TFR	INHERENT	7	2	31	LEAY		4	2
07	ASR		6	2	20	BRA	RELATIVE	3	2	32	LEAS		4	2
08	ASL/LSL		6	2	21	BRN		3	2	33	LEAU	INDEXED	4	2
09	ROL		6	2	22	BHI		3	2	34	PSHS	INHERENT	5	2
0A	DEC		6	2	23	BLS		3	2	35	PULS		5	2
0C	INC		6	2	24	BHS/BCC		3	2	36	PSHU		5	2
0D	TST		6	2	25	BLO/BCS		3	2	37	PULU		5	2
0E	JMP		3	2	26	BNE		3	2	39	RTS		5	1
0F	CLR	DIRECT	6	2	27	BEQ		3	2	3A	ABX		3	1
12	NOP	INHERENT	2	1	28	BVC		3	2	3B	RTI		6/15	1
13	SYNC	INHERENT	2	1	29	BVS		3	2	3C	CWAI		21	2
16	LBRA	RELATIVE	5	3	2A	BPL		3	2	3D	MUL		11	1
17	LBSR	RELATIVE	9	3	2B	BMI		3	2	3F	SWI		19	1
19	DAA	INHERENT	2	1	2C	BGE		3	2	40	NEGA		2	1
1A	ORCC	IMMED	3	2	2D	BLT	RELATIVE	3	2	43	COMA	INHERENT	2	1

OP	MNEM	MODE	~	#	OP	MNEM	MODE	~	#	OP	MNEM	MODE	~	#
44	LSRA	INHERENT	2	1	5D	TSTB	INHERENT	2	1	77	ASR	EXTENDED	7	3
46	RORA		2	1	5F	CLRB	INHERENT	2	1	78	ASL/LSL		7	3
47	ASRA		2	1	60	NEG	INDEXED	6	2	79	ROL		7	3
48	ASLA/LSLA		2	1	63	COM		6	2	7A	DEC		7	3
49	ROLA		2	1	64	LSR		6	2	7C	INC		7	3
4A	DECA		2	1	66	ROR		6	2	7D	TST		7	3
4C	INCA		2	1	67	ASR		6	2	7E	JMP		4	3
4D	TSTA		2	1	68	ASL/LSL		6	2	7F	CLR	EXTENDED	7	3
4F	CLRA		2	1	69	ROL		6	2	80	SUBA	IMMED	2	2
50	NEGB		2	1	6A	DEC		6	2	81	CMPA		2	2
53	COMB		2	1	6C	INC		6	2	82	SBCA		2	2
54	LSRB		2	1	6D	TST		6	2	83	SUBD		4	3
56	RORB		2	1	6E	JMP		3	2	84	ANDA		2	2
57	ASRA		2	1	6F	CLR	INDEXED	6	2	85	BITA		2	2
58	ASLB/LSLB		2	1	70	NEG	EXTENDED	7	3	86	LDA		2	2
59	ROLB		2	1	73	COM		7	3	88	EORA		2	2
5A	DECB		2	1	74	LSR		7	3	89	ADCA		2	2
5C	INCB	INHERENT	2	1	76	ROR	EXTENDED	7	3	8A	ORA	IMMED	2	2

OP	MNEM	MODE	~	#
8B	ADDA	IMMED	2	2
8C	CMPX	IMMED	4	3
8D	BSR	RELATIVE	7	2
8E	LDX	IMMED	3	3
90	SUBA	DIRECT	4	2
91	CMPA	DIRECT	4	2
92	SBCA	DIRECT	4	2
93	SUBD	DIRECT	6	2
94	ANDA	DIRECT	4	2
95	BITA	DIRECT	4	2
96	LDA	DIRECT	4	2
97	STA	DIRECT	4	2
98	EORA	DIRECT	4	2
99	ADCA	DIRECT	4	2
9A	ORA	DIRECT	4	2
9B	ADDA	DIRECT	4	2
9C	CMPX	DIRECT	6	2
9D	JSR	DIRECT	7	2
9E	LDX	DIRECT	5	2
9F	STX	DIRECT	5	2
A0	SUBA	INDEXED	4	2
A1	CMPA	INDEXED	4	2
A2	SBCA	INDEXED	4	2
A3	SUBD	INDEXED	6	2
A4	ANDA	INDEXED	4	2
A5	BITA	INDEXED	4	2
A6	LDA	INDEXED	4	2
A7	STA	INDEXED	4	2
A8	EORA	INDEXED	4	2
A9	ADCA	INDEXED	4	2
AA	ORA	INDEXED	4	2
AB	ADDA	INDEXED	4	2
AC	CMPX	INDEXED	6	2
AD	JSR	INDEXED	7	2
AE	LDX	INDEXED	5	2
AF	STX	INDEXED	5	2
B0	SUBA	EXTENDED	5	3
B1	CMPA	EXTENDED	5	3
B2	SBCA	EXTENDED	5	3
B3	SUBD	EXTENDED	7	3
B4	ANDA	EXTENDED	5	3
B5	BITA	EXTENDED	5	3
B6	LDA	EXTENDED	5	3
B7	STA	EXTENDED	5	3
B8	EORA	EXTENDED	5	3
B9	ADCA	EXTENDED	5	3
BA	ORA	EXTENDED	5	3
BB	ADDA	EXTENDED	5	3
BC	CMPX	EXTENDED	7	3
BD	JSR	EXTENDED	8	3
BE	LDX	EXTENDED	6	3
BF	STX	EXTENDED	6	3
C0	SUBB	IMMED	2	2
C1	CMPB	IMMED	2	2

OP	MNEM	MODE	~	#
C2	SBCB	IMMED	2	2
C3	ADDD	IMMED	4	3
C4	ANDB	IMMED	2	2
C5	BITB	IMMED	2	2
C6	LDB	IMMED	2	2
C8	EORB	IMMED	2	2
C9	ADCB	IMMED	2	2
CA	ORB	IMMED	2	2
CB	ADDB	IMMED	2	2
CC	LDD	IMMED	3	3
CE	LDU	IMMED	3	3
D0	SUBB	DIRECT	4	2
D1	CMPB	DIRECT	4	2
D2	SBCB	DIRECT	4	2
D3	ADDD	DIRECT	6	2
D4	ANDB	DIRECT	4	2
D5	BITB	DIRECT	4	2
D6	LDB	DIRECT	4	2
D7	STB	DIRECT	4	2
D8	EORB	DIRECT	4	2
D9	ADCB	DIRECT	4	2
DA	ORB	DIRECT	4	2
DB	ADDB	DIRECT	4	2
DC	LDD	DIRECT	5	2
DD	STD	DIRECT	5	2
DE	LDU	DIRECT	5	2
DF	STU	DIRECT	5	2
E0	SUBB	INDEXED	4	2
E1	CMPB	INDEXED	4	2
E2	SBCB	INDEXED	4	2
E3	ADDD	INDEXED	6	2
E4	ANDB	INDEXED	4	2
E5	BITB	INDEXED	4	2
E6	LDB	INDEXED	4	2
E7	STB	INDEXED	4	2
E8	EORB	INDEXED	4	2
E9	ADCB	INDEXED	4	2
EA	ORB	INDEXED	4	2
EB	ADDB	INDEXED	4	2
EC	LDD	INDEXED	5	2
ED	STD	INDEXED	5	2
EE	LDU	INDEXED	5	2
EF	STU	INDEXED	5	2
F0	SUBB	EXTENDED	5	3
F1	CMPB	EXTENDED	5	3
F2	SBCB	EXTENDED	5	3
F3	ADDD	EXTENDED	7	3
F4	ANDB	EXTENDED	5	3
F5	BITB	EXTENDED	5	3
F6	LDB	EXTENDED	5	3
F7	STB	EXTENDED	5	3
F8	EORB	EXTENDED	5	3
F9	ADCB	EXTENDED	5	3
FA	ORB	EXTENDED	5	3

OP	MNEM	MODE	~	#
FB	ADDB	EXTENDED	5	3
FC	LDD	EXTENDED	6	3
FD	STD	EXTENDED	6	3
FE	LDU	EXTENDED	6	3
FF	STU	EXTENDED	6	3
1021	LBRN	RELATIVE	5	4
1022	LBHI	RELATIVE	5(6)	4
1023	LBLS	RELATIVE	5(6)	4
1024	LBHS/LBCC	RELATIVE	5(6)	4
1025	LBCS/LBLO	RELATIVE	5(6)	4
1026	LBNE	RELATIVE	5(6)	4
1027	LBEQ	RELATIVE	5(6)	4
1028	LBVC	RELATIVE	5(6)	4
1029	LBVS	RELATIVE	5(6)	4
102A	LBPL	RELATIVE	5(6)	4
102B	LBMI	RELATIVE	5(6)	4
102C	LBGE	RELATIVE	5(6)	4
102D	LBLT	RELATIVE	5(6)	4
102E	LBGT	RELATIVE	5(6)	4
102F	LBLE	RELATIVE	5(6)	4
103F	SWI/2	INHERENT	20	2
1083	CMPD	IMMED	5	4
108C	CMPY	IMMED	5	4
108E	LDY	IMMED	4	4
1093	CMPD	DIRECT	7	3
109C	CMPY	DIRECT	7	3
109E	LDY	DIRECT	6	3
109F	STY	DIRECT	6	3
10A3	CMPD	INDEXED	7	3
10AC	CMPY	INDEXED	7	3
10AE	LDY	INDEXED	6	3
10AF	STY	INDEXED	6	3
10B3	CMPD	EXTENDED	8	4
10BC	CMPY	EXTENDED	8	4
10BE	LDY	EXTENDED	7	4
10BF	STY	EXTENDED	7	4
10CE	LDS	IMMED	4	4
10DE	LDS	DIRECT	6	3
10DF	STS	DIRECT	6	3
10EE	LDS	INDEXED	6	3
10EF	STS	INDEXED	6	3
10FE	LDS	EXTENDED	7	4
10FF	STS	EXTENDED	7	4
113F	SWI/3	INHERENT	20	2
1183	CMPU	IMMED	5	4
118C	CMPS	IMMED	5	4
1193	CMPU	DIRECT	7	3
119C	CMPS	DIRECT	7	3
11A3	CMPU	INDEXED	7	3
11AC	CMPS	INDEXED	7	3
11B3	CMPU	EXTENDED	8	4
11BC	CMPS	EXTENDED	8	4

INDEXED ADDRESSING POST BYTE REGISTER BIT ASSIGNMENTS

POST-BYTE REGISTER BIT								INDEXED ADDRESSING MODE
7	6	5	4	3	2	1	0	
0	X	X	X	X	X	X	X	EA = ,R ± 4 BIT OFFSET
1	X	X	0	0	0	0	0	,R+
1	X	X	X	0	0	0	1	,R++
1	X	X	0	0	0	1	0	,−R
1	X	X	X	0	0	1	1	,−−R
1	X	X	X	0	1	0	0	EA = ,R ± 0 OFFSET
1	X	X	X	0	1	0	1	EA = ,R ± ACCB OFFSET
1	X	X	X	0	1	1	0	EA = ,R ± ACCA OFFSET
1	X	X	X	1	0	0	0	EA = ,R ± 7 BIT OFFSET
1	X	X	X	1	0	0	1	EA = ,R ± 15 BIT OFFSET
1	X	X	X	1	0	1	1	EA = ,R ± D OFFSET)
1	X	X	X	1	1	0	0	EA = ,PC ± 7 BIT OFFSET
1	X	X	X	1	1	0	1	EA = ,PC ± 15 BIT OFFSET
1	X	X	1	1	1	1	1	EA = ,ADDRESS

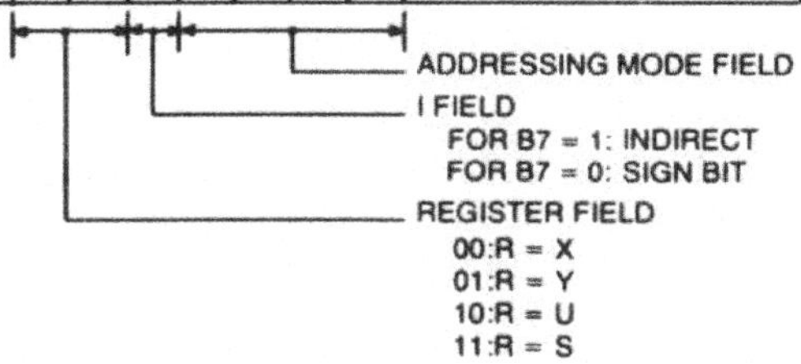

PUSH/PULL POST BYTE

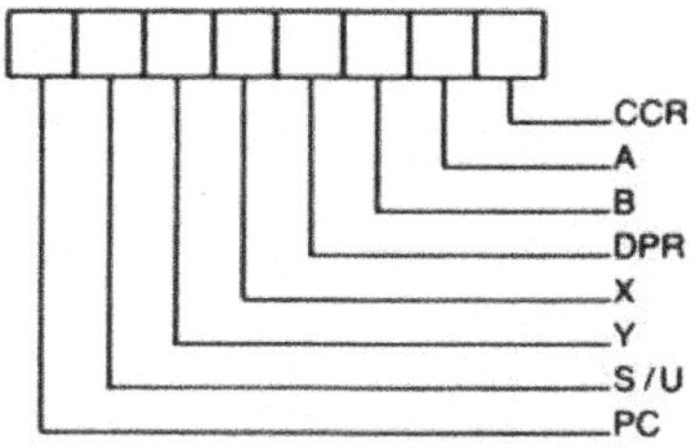

TRANSFER/EXCHANGE POST BYTE

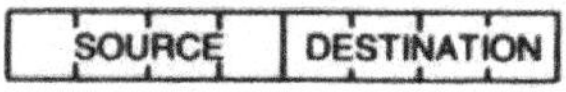

REGISTER FIELD

0000 = D (A:B)	1000 = A
0001 = X	1001 = B
0010 = Y	1010 = CCR
0011 = U	1011 = DPR
0100 = S	
0101 = PC	

6809 STACKING ORDER

PULL ORDER
↓
CC
A
B
DP
X Hi
X Lo
Y Hi
Y Lo
U/S Hi
U/S Lo
PC Hi
PC Lo
↑
PUSH ORDER

INCREASING MEMORY
↓

6809 VECTORS

FFFE	Restart
FFFC	NMI
FFFA	SWI
FFF8	IRQ
FFF6	FIRQ
FFF4	SWI2
FFF2	SWI3
FFF0	Reserved

INDEXED ADDRESSING MODES

TYPE	FORMS	NON INDIRECT Assembler Form	NON INDIRECT Post-Byte OP Code	+ ~	+ #	INDIRECT Assembler Form	INDIRECT Post-Byte OP Code	+ ~	+ #
CONSTANT OFFSET FROM R	NO OFFSET	, R	1RR00100	0	0	[, R]	1RR10100	3	0
	5 BIT OFFSET	n, R	0RRnnnnn	1	0	defaults to 8-bit			
	8 BIT OFFSET	n, R	1RR01000	1	1	[n, R]	1RR11000	4	1
	16 BIT OFFSET	n, R	1RR01001	4	2	[n, R]	1RR11001	7	2
ACCUMULATOR OFFSET FROM R	A—REGISTER OFFSET	A, R	1RR00110	1	0	[A, R]	1RR10110	4	0
	B—REGISTER OFFSET	B, R	1RR00101	1	0	[B, R]	1RR10101	4	0
	D—REGISTER OFFSET	D, R	1RR01011	4	0	[D, R]	1RR11011	7	0
AUTO INCREMENT/DECREMENT R	INCREMENT BY 1	, R+	1RR00000	2	0	not allowed			
	INCREMENT BY 2	, R++	1RR00001	3	0	[, R++]	1RR10001	6	0
	DECREMENT BY 1	, −R	1RR00010	2	0	not allowed			
	DECREMENT BY 2	, −−R	1RR00011	3	0	[, −−R]	1RR10011	6	0
CONSTANT OFFSET FROM PC	8 BIT OFFSET	n, PCR	1XX01100	1	1	[n, PCR]	1XX11100	4	1
	16 BIT OFFSET	n, PCR	1XX01101	5	2	[n, PCR]	1XX11101	8	2
EXTENDED INDIRECT	16 BIT ADDRESS	—	—	-	-	[n]	10011111	5	2

R = X, Y, U, or S
X = DON'T CARE

NOTES:

1. Given in the table are the base cycles and byte counts. To determine the total cycles and byte counts add the values from the '6809 indexing modes' table.
2. R1 and R2 may be any pair of 8 bit or any pair of 16 bit registers.
   The 8 bit registers are: A, B, CC, DP
   The 16 bit registers are: X, Y, U, S, D, PC
3. EA is the effective address.
4. The PSH and PUL instructions require 5 cycles plus 1 cycle for each *byte* pushed or pulled.
5. 5(6) means: 5 cycles if branch not taken, 6 cycles if taken.
6. SW1 sets I&F bits. SW12 and SW13 do not affect I&F.
7. Conditions Codes set as a direct result of the instruction.
8. Value of half-carry flag is undefined.
9. Special Case—Carry set if b7 is SET.

LEGEND:

OP	Operation Code (Hexadecimal);	Z	Zero (byte)
~	Number of MPU Cycles;	V	Overflow, 2's complement
#	Number of Program Bytes;	C	Carry from bit 7
+	Arithmetic Plus;	↕	Test and set if true, cleared otherwise
−	Arithmetic Minus;	•	Not Affected
·	Multiply	CC	Condition Code Register
$\overline{M}$	Complement of M;	:	Concatenation
→	Transfer Into;	∨	Logical or
H	Half-carry from bit 3;	∧	Logical and
N	Negative (sign bit)	⊻	Logical Exclusive or

INSTRUCTION/		INHERENT			DIRECT			EXTENDED			IMMEDIATE			INDEXED[1]			RELATIVE				5	3	2	1	0
	FORMS	OP	~	#	OP	~	#	OP	~	#	OP	~	#	OP	~	#	OP	~[5]	#	DESCRIPTION	H	N	Z	V	C
ABX		3A	3	1																B + X → X (UNSIGNED)	•	•	•	•	•
ADC	ADCA				99	4	2	B9	5	3	89	2	2	A9	4+	2+				A + M + C → A	↕	↕	↕	↕	↕
	ADCB				D9	4	2	F9	5	3	C9	2	2	E9	4+	2+				B + M + C → B	↕	↕	↕	↕	↕
ADD	ADDA				9B	4	2	BB	5	3	8B	2	2	AB	4+	2+				A + M → A	↕	↕	↕	↕	↕
	ADDB				DB	4	2	FB	5	3	CB	2	2	EB	4+	2+				B + M → B	↕	↕	↕	↕	↕
	ADDD				D3	6	2	F3	7	3	C3	4	3	E3	6+	2+				D + M:M + 1 → D	↕	↕	↕	↕	↕
AND	ANDA				94	4	2	B4	5	3	84	2	2	A4	4+	2+				A ∧ M → A	•	↕	↕	0	•
	ANDB				D4	4	2	F4	5	3	C4	2	2	E4	4+	2+				B ∧ M → B	•	↕	↕	0	•
	ANDCC										1C	3	2							CC ∧ IMM → CC					1
ASL	ASLA	48	2	1																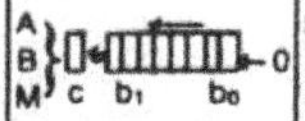	8	↕	↕	↕	↕
	ASLB	58	2	1																	8	↕	↕	↕	↕
	ASL				08	6	2	78	7	3				68	6+	2+					8	↕	↕	↕	↕
ASR	ASRA	47	2	1																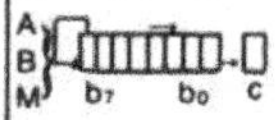	8	↕	↕	•	↕
	ASR	57	2	1																	8	↕	↕	•	↕
	ASR				07	6	2	77	7	3				67	6+	2+					8	↕	↕	•	↕
BCC	BCC																24	3	2	Branch C = 0	•	•	•	•	•
	LBCC																10 24	5(6)	4	Long Branch C = 0	•	•	•	•	•
BCS	BCS																25	3	2	Branch C = 1	•	•	•	•	•
	LBCS																10 25	5(6)	4	Long Branch C = 1	•	•	•	•	•
BEQ	BEQ																27	3	2	Branch Z = 0	•	•	•	•	•
	LBEQ																10 27	5(6)	4	Long Branch Z = 0	•	•	•	•	•
BGE	BGE																2C	3	2	Branch ≥ Zero	•	•	•	•	•
	LBGE																10 2C	5(6)	4	Long Branch ≥ Zero	•	•	•	•	•
BGT	BGT																2E	3	2	Branch > Zero	•	•	•	•	•
	LBGT																10 2E	5(6)	4	Long Branch > Zero	•	•	•	•	•
BHI	BHI																22	3	2	Branch Higher	•	•	•	•	•
	LBHI																10 22	5(6)	4	Long Branch Higher	•	•	•	•	•
BHS	BHS																24	3	2	Branch Higher or Same	•	•	•	•	•
	LBHS																10 24	5(6)	4	Long Branch Higher or Same	•	•	•	•	•
BIT	BITA				95	4	2	B5	5	3	85	2	2	A5	4+	2+				Bit Test A (M ∧ A)	•	↕	↕	0	•
	BITB				D5	4	2	F5	5	3	C5	2	2	E5	4+	2+				Bit Test B (M ∧ B)	•	↕	↕	0	•
BLE	BLE																2F	3	2	Branch ≤ Zero	•	•	•	•	•
	LBLE																10 2F	5(6)	4	Long Branch ≤ Zero	•	•	•	•	•
BLO	BLO																25	3	2	Branch Lower	•	•	•	•	•
	LBLO																10 25	5(6)	4	Long Branch Lower	•	•	•	•	•
BLS	BLS																23	3	2	Branch Lower or Same	•	•	•	•	•
	LBLS																10 23	5(6)	4	Long Branch Lower or Same	•	•	•	•	•
BLT	BLT																2D	3	2	Branch < Zero	•	•	•	•	•
	LBLT																10 2D	5(6)	4	Long Branch < Zero	•	•	•	•	•
BMI	BMI																2B	3	2	Branch Minus	•	•	•	•	•
	LBMI																10 2B	5(6)	4	Long Branch Minus	•	•	•	•	•
BNE	BNE																26	3	2	Branch Z ≠ 0	•	•	•	•	•
	LBNE																10 26	5(6)	4	Long Branch Z ≠ 0	•	•	•	•	•
BPL	BPL																2A	3	2	Branch Plus	•	•	•	•	•
	LBPL																10 2A	5(6)	4	Long Branch Plus	•	•	•	•	•

INSTRUCTION/	FORMS	INHERENT			DIRECT			EXTENDED			IMMEDIATE			INDEXED[1]			RELATIVE				5	3	2	1	0
		OP	~	#	OP	~	#	OP	~	#	OP	~	#	OP	~	#	OP	~[5]	#	DESCRIPTION	H	N	Z	V	C
BRA	BRA																20	3	2	Branch Always	•	•	•	•	•
	LBRA																16	5	3	Long Branch Always	•	•	•	•	•
BRN	BRN																21	3	2	Branch Never	•	•	•	•	•
	LBRN																10 21	5	4	Long Branch Never	•	•	•	•	•
BSR	BSR																8D	7	2	Branch to Subroutine	•	•	•	•	•
	LBSR																17	9	3	Long Branch to Subroutine	•	•	•	•	•
BVC	BVC																28	3	2	Branch V = 0	•	•	•	•	•
	LBVC																10 28	5(6)	4	Long Branch V = 0	•	•	•	•	•
BVS	BVS																29	3	2	Branch V = 1	•	•	•	•	•
	LBVS																10 29	5(6)	4	Long Branch V = 1	•	•	•	•	•
CLR	CLRA	4F	2	1																0 → A	•	0	1	0	0
	CLRB	5F	2	1																0 → B	•	0	1	0	0
	CLR				0F	6	2	7F	7	3				6F	6+	2+				0 → M	•	0	1	0	0
CMP	CMPA				91	4	2	B1	5	3	81	2	2	A1	4+	2+				Compare M from A	8	↕	↕	↕	↕
	CMPB				D1	4	2	F1	5	3	C1	2	2	E1	4+	2+				Compare M from B	8	↕	↕	↕	↕
	CMPD				10 93	7	3	10 B3	8	4	10 83	5	4	10 A3	7+	3+				Compare M: M + 1 from D	•	↕	↕	↕	↕
	CMPS				11 9C	7	3	11 BC	8	4	11 8C	5	4	11 AC	7+	3+				Compare M: M + 1 from S	•	↕	↕	↕	↕
	CMPU				11 93	7	3	11 B3	8	4	11 83	5	4	11 A3	7+	3+				Compare M: M + 1 from U	•	↕	↕	↕	↕
	CMPX				9C	6	2	BC	7	3	8C	4	3	AC	6+	2+				Compare M: M + 1 from X	•	↕	↕	↕	↕
	CMPY				10 9C	7	3	10 BC	8	4	10 8C	5	4	10 AC	7+	3+				Compare M: M + 1 from Y	•	↕	↕	↕	↕
COM	COMA	43	2	1																$\overline{A}$ → A	•	↕	↕	0	1
	COMB	53	2	1																$\overline{B}$ → B	•	↕	↕	0	1
	COM				03	6	2	73	7	3				63	6+	2+				$\overline{M}$ → M	•	↕	↕	0	1
CWAI		3C	20	2																CC IMM → CC: Wait for Interrupt					1
DAA		19	2	1																Decimal Adjust A	•	↕	↕	0	↕
DEC	DECA	4A	2	1																A − 1 → A	•	↕	↕	↕	•
	DECB	5A	2	1																B − 1 → B	•	↕	↕	↕	•
	DEC				0A	6	2	7A	7	3				6A	6+	2+				M − 1 → M	•	↕	↕	↕	•
EOR	EORA				98	4	2	B8	5	3	88	2	2	A8	4+	2+				A ⊻ M → A	•	↕	↕	0	•
	EORB				D8	4	2	F8	5	3	C8	2	2	E8	4+	2+				B ⊻ M → B	•	↕	↕	0	•
EXG	R1, R2	1E	7	2																R1 ↔ R2[2]	•	•	•	•	•
INC	INCA	4C	2	1																A + 1 → A	•	↕	↕	↕	•
	INCB	5C	2	1																B + 1 → B	•	↕	↕	↕	•
	INC				0C	6	2	7C	7	3				6C	6+	2+				M + 1 → M	•	↕	↕	↕	•
JMP					0E	3	2	7E	4	3				6E	3+	2+				EA[3] → PC	•	•	•	•	•
JSR					9D	7	2	BD	8	3				AD	7+	2+				Jump to Subroutine	•	•	•	•	•
LD	LDA				96	4	2	B6	5	3	86	2	2	A6	4+	2+				M → A	•	↕	↕	0	•
	LDB				D6	4	2	F6	5	3	C6	2	2	E6	4+	2+				M → B	•	↕	↕	0	•
	LDD				DC	5	2	FC	6	3	CC	3	3	EC	5+	2+				M: M + 1 → D	•	↕	↕	0	•
	LDS				10 DE	6	3	10 FE	7	4	10 CE	4	4	10 EE	6+	3+				M: M + 1 → S	•	↕	↕	0	•
	LDU				DE	5	2	FE	6	3	CE	3	3	EE	5+	2+				M: M + 1 → U	•	↕	↕	0	•
	LDX				9E	5	2	BE	6	3	8E	3	3	AE	5+	2+				M: M + 1 → X	•	↕	↕	0	•
	LDY				10 9E	6	3	10 BE	7	4	10 8E	4	4	10 AE	6+	3+				M: M + 1 → Y	•	↕	↕	0	•
LEA	LEAS													32	4+	2+				EA[3] → S	•	•	•	•	•
	LEAU													33	4+	2+				EA[3] → U	•	•	•	•	•
	LEAX													30	4+	2+				EA[3] → X	•	•	↕	•	•
	LEAY													31	4+	2+				EA[3] → Y	•	•	↕	•	•

INSTRUCTION/	FORMS	INHERENT			DIRECT			EXTENDED			IMMEDIATE			INDEXED[1]			RELATIVE				5	3	2	1	0
		OP	~	#	OP	~	#	OP	~	#	OP	~	#	OP	~	#	OP	~[5]	#	DESCRIPTION	H	N	Z	V	C
LSL	LSLA	48	2	1																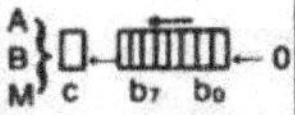	•	↕	↕	↕	↕
	LSLB	58	2	1																	•	↕	↕	↕	↕
	LSL				08	6	2	78	7	3				68	6+	2+					•	↕	↕	↕	↕
LSR	LSRA	44	2	1																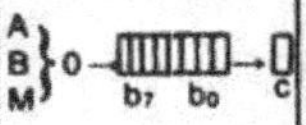	•	0	↕	•	↕
	LSRB	54	2	1																	•	0	↕	•	↕
	LSR				04	6	2	74	7	3				64	6+	2+					•	0	↕	•	↕
MUL		3D	11	1																A × B → D (Unsigned)	•	•	↕	•	9
NEG	NEGA	40	2	1																$\overline{A}$ + 1 → A	8	↕	↕	↕	↕
	NEGB	50	2	1																$\overline{B}$ + 1 → B	8	↕	↕	↕	↕
	NEG				00	6	2	70	7	3				60	6+	2+				$\overline{M}$ + 1 → M	8	↕	↕	↕	↕
NOP		12	2	1																No Operation	•	•	•	•	•
OR	ORA				9A	4	2	BA	5	3	8A	2	2	AA	4+	2+				A ∨ M → A	•	↕	↕	0	•
	ORB				DA	4	2	FA	5	3	CA	2	2	EA	4+	2+				B ∨ M → B	•	↕	↕	0	•
	ORCC										1A	3	2							CC ∨ IMM → CC					7
PSH	PSHS	34	5+[4]	2																Push Registers on S Stack	•	•	•	•	•
	PSHU	36	5+[4]	2																Push Registers on U Stack	•	•	•	•	•
PUL	PULS	35	5+[4]	2																Pull Registers from S Stack	•	•	•	•	•
	PULU	37	5+[4]	2																Pull Registers from U Stack	•	•	•	•	•
ROL	ROLA	49	2	1																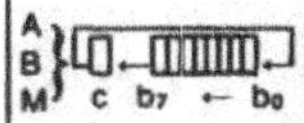	•	↕	↕	↕	↕
	ROLB	59	2	1																	•	↕	↕	↕	↕
	ROL				09	6	2	79	7	3				69	6+	2+					•	↕	↕	↕	↕
ROR	RORA	46	2	1																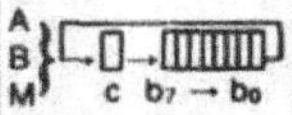	•	↕	↕	•	↕
	RORB	56	2	1																	•	↕	↕	•	↕
	ROR				06	6	2	76	7	3				66	6+	2+					•	↕	↕	•	↕
RTI		3B	6/15	1																Return From Interrupt					7
RTS		39	5	1																Return From Subroutine	•	•	•	•	•
SBC	SBCA				92	4	2	B2	5	3	82	2	2	A2	4+	2+				A − M − C → A	8	↕	↕	↕	↕
	SBCB				D2	4	2	F2	5	3	C2	2	2	E2	4+	2+				B − M − C → B	8	↕	↕	↕	↕
SEX		1D	2	1																Sign Extend B into A	•	↕	↕	0	•
ST	STA				97	4	2	B7	5	3				A7	4+	2+				A → M	•	↕	↕	0	•
	STB				D7	4	2	F7	5	3				E7	4+	2+				B → M	•	↕	↕	0	•
	STD				DD	5	2	FD	6	3				ED	5+	2+				D → M: M + 1	•	↕	↕	0	•
	STS				10	6	3	10	7	4				10	6+	3+				S → M: M + 1	•	↕	↕	0	•
					DF			FF						EF											
	STU				DF	5	2	FF	6	3				EF	5+	2+				U → M: M + 1	•	↕	↕	0	•
	STX				9F	5	2	BF	6	3				AF	5+	2+				X → M: M + 1	•	↕	↕	0	•
	STY				10	6	3	10	7	4				10						Y → M: M + 1	•	↕	↕	0	•
					9F			BF						AF	6+	3+									
SUB	SUBA				90	4	2	B0	5	3	80	2	2	A0	4+	2+				A − M → A	8	↕	↕	↕	↕
	SUBB				D0	4	2	F0	5	3	C0	2	2	E0	4+	2+				B − M → B	8	↕	↕	↕	↕
	SUBD				93	6	2	B3	7	3	83	4	3	A3	6+	2+				D − M: M + 1 → D	•	↕	↕	↕	↕
SWI	SWI[6]	3F	19	1																Software Interrupt 1	•	•	•	•	•
	SWI2[6]	10 3F	20	2																Software Interrupt 2	•	•	•	•	•
	SWI3[6]	11 3F	20	2																Software Interrupt 3	•	•	•	•	•
SYNC		13	≥2	1																Synchronize to Interrupt	•	•	•	•	•
TFR	R1, R2	1F	7	2																R1 → R2[2]	•	•	•	•	•
TST	TSTA	4D	2	1																Test A	•	↕	↕	0	•
	TSTB	5D	2	1																Test B	•	↕	↕	0	•
	TST				0D	6	2	7D	7	3				6D	6+	2+				Test M	•	↕	↕	0	•

Made in the USA
Monee, IL
08 November 2026

67379941R10090